GED

Contemporary

Foundations

Reading

PROJECT SECOND CHANCE
CONTRA COSTA COUNTY LIBRARY

D0817464

Mc Graw Hill **Wright Group**

The McGraw·Hill Companies

www.WrightGroup.com

Wright Group

Printed in the United States of America

Send all inquiries to:
McGraw-Hill/Contemporary
P. O. Box 812960
Chicago, IL 60681

ISBN: 978-1-4045-7633-9
MHID: 1-4045-7633-9

1 2 3 4 5 6 7 8 9 10 COU 12 11 10 09 08

The McGraw·Hill Companies

CONTENTS

Contents

ACKNOWLEDGMENTS

Photo on page 2, © Getty Images

Photo on page 30, © Bruce Laurance/The Image Bank/Getty Images

Photo on page 50, © Alan C. Helson/Shutterstock Images LLC

Photo on page 51, © Veer

Cartoon on page 57, John Darkow, 1992, *Columbia Daily Tribune*. Reprinted by permission of the John Darkow.

Cartoon on page 58, © Piero Tonin/Cartoonstock

Cartoon on page 59, © Stan Eales/Cartoonstock

Cartoon on page 60, © Betsy Streeter/Cartoonstock

Cartoon on page 61, © Jerry King/Cartoon stock

Cartoon on page 62, Arlo & Janis Cartoon "That's a Pretty Salad You've Made!" by Jimmy Johnson, 4/9/1992. Arlo and Janis: © Newspaper Enterprise Association, Inc.

Photo on page 66, © Juice Images/Punchstock

Poem on page 68, "Fog" from *Chicago Poems* by Carl Sandburg, copyright 1916 by Holt, Rinehart and Winston and renewed 1944 by Carl Sandburg, reprinted by permission of Harcourt Inc.

Poem on page 69, "Concrete Cat" by Dorthi Charles, from *An Introduction to Poetry, 12th edition* by X.J. Kennedy and Dana Gioia. Reprinted by permission of X.J. Kennedy.

Poem on page 70, "Well, Yes" by Robert Froman. Copyright © 1974 by Robert Froman. First appeared in *Seeing Things: A Book Of Poems*, published by Thomas Y. Crowell. Reprinted by permission of Curtis Brown, Ltd.

Poem on page 72, "We Real Cool" by Gwendolyn Brooks. Reprinted By Consent of Brooks Permissions.

Poem on page 74, "A Seeing Poem" by Robert Froman. Copyright © 1971 by Robert Froman. First appeared in *Street Poems*, published by Thomas Y. Crowell. Reprinted by permission of Curtis Brown, Ltd.

Poem on page 84, "Dust of Snow" by Robert Frost from *The Poetry of Robert Frost* edited by Edward Connery Lathem.

Poem on page 80, "Steam Shovel" by Charles Malam from *Upper Pasture*, 1930.

Poem on page 82, "Daddy Fell into the Pond" by Alfred Noyes. The Society of Authors as the Literary Representative of the Estate of Alfred Noyes. Reprinted by permission.

Introduction

Welcome to Contemporary's *Foundations: Reading*. This book will help you improve your reading. It will also help you improve your writing and thinking skills.

This book is divided into four units.

Practical Reading—"survival" reading that you do everyday. Practical reading includes instructions, advertisements, and explanations.

Reading Nonfiction—writing based on facts. Nonfiction includes newspaper and magazine articles, books about real people and real events, and encyclopedia articles.

Reading Poetry—verse that captures a person's feelings. Learning to recognize form, rhythm, rhyme, and images will help you read and appreciate poetry.

Reading Short Fiction—stories created from an author's imagination. Characters, setting, plot, and theme are important elements in every story.

These special features in *Foundations: Reading* will help you practice your language skills.

Writing Workshops—detailed instructions that will guide you through the four-step writing process: prewriting, drafting, revising, and editing

Language Tips—explanations, pronunciations, study hints, and background information that will help you understand what you are reading

Test Skills—a reminder that this skill is often tested on standardized tests

Posttest—a test, evaluation chart, and answer key so you will know how well you have mastered the skills

We hope you will enjoy *Foundations: Reading*. We wish you the best of luck with your studies!

Foundations

Contemporary's *Foundations* is a series of books designed to help you improve your skills. Each book provides skill instruction, offers interesting passages to study, and gives opportunities to practice what you are learning.

In addition to *Foundations: Reading,* we invite you to explore these books.

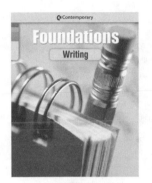

- In *Foundations: Writing,* you will practice the four steps to writing an essay: **prewriting, drafting, revising,** and **editing.**
- You will read and write five kinds of essays—**descriptive essays, personal narratives, how-to essays, essays of example,** and **comparison-and-contrast essays.**
- A language-skills workbook gives you **grammar, punctuation,** and **sentence structure** practice.
- **In Your Journal, With a Partner,** and **Language Tips** will help you become a better writer—and a better reader and thinker.

- In *Foundations: Science,* you will learn about the **human body, plant biology, physics, chemistry,** and **Earth science.**
- You will practice putting events in **order;** reading **diagrams, charts,** and **graphs;** using the **scientific method;** and making **comparisons and contrasts.**
- **Try It Yourself!** activities will guide you through simple experiments so you will have a better understanding of what you have been reading about. **Writing Workshops** and **Language Tips** will help you use your reading and writing skills to think about science topics.

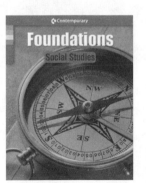

- In *Foundations: Social Studies,* you will learn about **world history, U.S. history, civics and government, geography,** and **economics.**
- You will **summarize,** make **predictions,** infer the main idea of **cartoons,** find information on **maps,** and read various kinds of **graphs.**
- **Background Information, Language Tips,** and **Writing Workshops** will let you use what you already know as you read and write about social studies topics.

- In *Foundations: Math,* you will practice using **whole numbers, money, decimals, fractions, ratios,** and **percents.**
- Exercises will help you review the **addition, subtraction, multiplication,** and **division** facts; **round numbers; estimate** answers; and solve **word problems.**
- **Math Notes, On Your Calculator,** and **Language Tips** will help you improve your math skills.

UNIT 1
Practical Reading

PRACTICAL READING is what you might call "survival" reading. It is the kind of reading you do every day to get the information you need to function well at work, at home, and in our society.

Newspapers provide good opportunities for practical reading. They tell you everything from who is running for political office to what time your local theater is showing the movie you want to see. Practical reading also includes reading recipes, instructions for recording TV programs, and the lease you sign when you rent an apartment.

Chapter	What You Will Learn About	What You Will Read
1	Main Idea	Planning Ahead for Car Emergencies Using Your Microwave Oven Keeping a Nontoxic House Juggling Daycare and a Job
2	Details	Flea Market Sale Making an Emergency Kit Shopping in a Mall Looking for an Apartment
3	Time Order	Time to Plant Tomatoes Painting a Room The Automated Teller Machine Aerobic Exercise Session
Review	Practical Reading	Giving Blood

After reading this unit, you should be able to

- find the main idea
- find details
- follow time order in instructions

Main Idea

Newspaper reporters write about people and events that will interest their readers. When you read a newspaper or magazine, the headlines are probably the first thing you notice.

Crime Rate Increases
Air Pollution Controls Needed
Rain and Snow at Super Bowl

A headline announces the **topic** of a news story. From the headline, you can predict what the news story is about. You expect that the story gives you information about the topic mentioned in the headline.

The **main idea** of a news story is a general statement telling the most important point that the writer wants you to understand about the topic. For example, in a news story about increasing crime rates, the main idea might be "Most major U.S. cities experienced increased robberies and murders last year." In a news story about air pollution, the main idea might be "The health of our children depends on stricter air pollution controls."

Planning Ahead for Car Emergencies

When a driving emergency happens, you will not have time to look up information in a book about what you should do. You will have to react right away. You should plan ahead so you will know the steps to take in a driving emergency. Knowing the following facts could save your life.

First, if a tire blows out, do not step on the brake pedal. Slowly release the accelerator. Then steer the car as straight as possible while applying gentle, even pressure to the brakes. Pull slowly off the road, stop in a safe place, and wait for help.

Second, if the car skids on ice, steer in the direction of the skid. If the wheels go off the road onto a low shoulder, brake gently. Ride the shoulder until you can turn up onto the road. If you try to jerk the car back onto the road, you're likely to continue skidding.

Third, if your brakes fail, apply the parking brake slowly but firmly. If you have time, shift the gears down (from drive to second to first). You may have time to shift to reverse. Never shift into park. If shifting does not bring the car to a halt, turn off the ignition. Do not turn the ignition to the lock position because that will lock the steering wheel in place. If all else fails, try to hit guardrails, fences, or signposts to slow the car.

You can avoid many emergencies by driving defensively. Always remember to buckle your seat belt, even if you are driving only a few blocks.

Look at how the article is organized. It has five paragraphs. The main idea of each paragraph is stated in the topic sentence. A topic sentence often—but not always—begins a paragraph. The other sentences in the paragraph support the main idea.

◆ **On the lines below, write the topic sentence of the first paragraph. What is the writer's most important point about driving emergencies?**

_____

_____

You are correct if you wrote **You should plan ahead so you will know the steps to take in a driving emergency.**

◆ **Go back and underline the topic sentence in the other four paragraphs.**

You should have underlined **the first sentence** in each of these paragraphs.

To find the main idea of the entire article, look at the topic sentences of the five paragraphs. Together, these sentences can help you figure out the writer's most important point. The main idea of this article is "Drivers should plan ahead for car emergencies."

Strategy: How to Find the Main Idea

- Read the entire article.
- Find the topic. What is the article about?
- Find the main idea. What is the writer's most important point?
- To be sure you have correctly identified the main idea, check that the details in each paragraph relate to that idea.

Exercise 1

Good instructions start with the main idea. Then they give you steps to follow. Have you used instructions to program a DVD player or connect a new car stereo? Did you think those instructions were easy to follow?

Read the instructions and answer the questions.

Using Your Microwave Oven

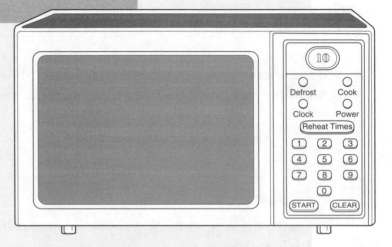

Read all the instructions carefully before using your new microwave oven. Each oven has its own control panel, but most microwave ovens operate in a similar way. Look at the control panel shown here. It displays the time at the top of the panel. Under the time are keys for various functions. You can press *Defrost, Cook, Clock,* or *Power.* You can also warm food by pressing *Reheat Times.*

Under the function keys are numbers. The numbers 0 through 9 are displayed like the numbers on a calculator. You press the numbers to set the cooking time in minutes and seconds. Under the numbers are the *Start* and *Clear* keys.

A microwave oven will automatically cook on HIGH (power level 10) unless you enter a lower power level. Suppose you want to cook a serving of broccoli for two and a half minutes on MEDIUM power (level 5). First, press the numbers 2, 3, and 0 (2 minutes and 30 seconds). Then, press *Power.* Next, press the number 5. Finally, press *Start* to begin cooking. If you make a mistake, press *Clear.* This will clear the display and allow you to start over again.

1. Write the main idea of this article.

   _____

2. What does the third paragraph tell you how to do?

   _____

   _____

3. What keys would you press to cook green beans for three minutes and twenty seconds at power level 7?

   _____

4. What is the last key you press each time you set the controls?

   _____

5. What does pressing *Clear* allow you to do?

   _____

Check your answers on page 158.

Do you worry about pollution inside your house? What products do you use to clean your house? Do they ever make your eyes sting or your hands hurt?

Read the article and complete the exercise.

Keeping a Nontoxic House

Many common cleaning products are **toxic.** They are made of powerful chemicals that can hurt you when you breathe them in or touch them. Most cleaners are stronger than they need to be. These cleaners can do more harm than good.

What steps can you take to avoid indoor pollution caused by cleaning products? First, read labels to identify cleaners that are dangerous. Second, if you must use strong cleaners, wear rubber gloves. Then you will not absorb the chemicals through your skin. Third, make your own milder cleaning supplies. Fourth, find books that give earth-friendly housecleaning tips.

One good book on the subject is *Clean & Green* by Annie Berthold-Bond. It includes a recipe for a mild yet effective all-purpose cleaner. You can make it with everyday ingredients you buy at your local supermarket. In a spray bottle, put 1 teaspoon of boric acid, ½ teaspoon of washing or sal soda, 2 tablespoons of vinegar or lemon juice, and ¼ teaspoon of liquid soap. Combine these ingredients, and then add 2 cups of very hot water. Shake the bottle gently until all the minerals dissolve. This solution will safely and thoroughly clean everything from vinyl floors to metal fixtures.

You can also breathe in toxic chemicals. Make sure your house is well ventilated during and after cleaning. If you are working in an unventialted room, take short breaks outside the room. In addition, vent your clothes dryer to the outdoors. Taking these steps will help make your house nontoxic.

---

toxic: poisonous

Match each question with its answer.

_____ 1. What is the topic of the article?

_____ 2. What is the main idea of paragraph 3?

_____ 3. What can you do to avoid contact with toxic chemicals?

_____ 4. How might dangerous chemicals get to you while you clean?

_____ 5. What can you clean with the mixture in the spray bottle?

_____ 6. What is the main idea of the article?

(a) read labels, wear rubber gloves, and learn about earth-friendly cleaning

(b) Indoor pollution can be avoided by using nontoxic cleaners.

(c) keeping a nontoxic house

(d) vinyl floors and metal fixtures

(e) A nontoxic cleaner can be made with everyday ingredients.

(f) They can be breathed in or absorbed through your skin.

Check your answers on page 158.

Exercise 3

Do you have children who go to daycare while you work? Do you think employers should help more with child care?

Read the article and answer the questions.

LANGUAGE Tip

Multiple Meanings

Perhaps you have seen a juggler throwing several objects into the air, catching them, and then tossing them up again. In this essay, *juggle* means "doing many things at a time."

Juggling Daycare and a Job

If you have young children and work outside your home, you know how hard it is to juggle work schedules and daycare. You have to drop off your children for daycare and still get to work on time. This is how one family does it.

Rosa works at an electronics company. Her husband, Bob, manages the mailroom for a medical equipment company. They have a six-year-old daughter and a two-year-old son. They live in Washington, D.C. Every day Bob drops off their daughter at a nearby grade school. Then he drives to his job, which is about thirty minutes away. Rosa takes their son downtown on the subway. She drops him off at a daycare center a few blocks from where she works.

Rosa and Bob both have to be flexible. If either parent has a late meeting or if either child needs to see a doctor, they have to change their schedules. "When something comes up, we have to create of a new plan," says Rosa. "Sometimes I think we will be living from one crisis to the next until our son is 18."

In 2001, 61% of mothers with children under age 6 worked outside their homes. Society and employers have not caught up with this reality. Only a small number of employers offer on-site daycare. However, a few companies have begun to offer job sharing for working parents. "Job sharing" means that two people share one full-time job. By working fewer hours, employees find it easier to take care of their children. Companies are starting to realize that such programs make good business sense. Their workers are more productive. There is less absenteeism, tardiness, and staff turnover. Job satisfaction is increased when families do not feel they are living from one crisis to the next.

1. What is the main idea of the article? _____

2. How do Bob and Rosa manage their work and daycare schedules?

   _____

3. What is the main idea of the last paragraph of the article? _____

   _____

4. What are some benefits to employers who provide child-care options?

   _____

Check your answers on page 158.

Writing Workshop

Prewriting
Choose an appliance or machine that you know how to use to describe to someone.

Drafting
Write a sentence stating the purpose of the appliance or machine. Add sentences that explain the topic sentence in more detail.

Revising
Be sure that your main idea is clearly stated. Check that each detail describes how the machine works or why it is helpful. You may work with a partner.

Editing
Be sure each sentence ends with a period, exclamation point, or question mark. Check the spelling of words you are not sure about.

Details

When news reporters research an article, they ask questions that begin with *who,* *what, where, when, why,* and *how.* The answers to these questions are often become the **details** of a news story. Details tell you more about the main idea.

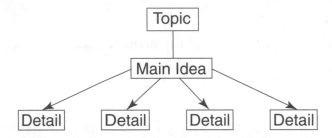

How can you use reporters' questions to improve your practical reading skills? As you read the poster below, ask yourself the questions *Who? What? Where? When? Why?* and *How?* Answering these questions will help you find the facts related to the main idea of the poster.

Flea Market Sale

Come One, Come All

FIRST ANNUAL CRABTREE FLEA MARKET!

It will be the biggest sale of the year! Great bargains on everything from china and picture frames to clothes and car tires. Prices start at $1. It's a sale you can't afford to miss!

❖ Sale items will be displayed at the Hi-Way Drive-in Theater, Route 30, 1 mile east of Crabtree.

❖ Saturday, June 20, from 9:00 a.m. until 9:00 p.m.

❖ Artists, farmers, and dealers from a three-state area will be selling their treasures.

❖ China, glassware, art, furniture, lamps, plant stands, books, homemade jams and jellies, pictures and frames, clothing, towels, jewelry, tools, garden supplies, car parts, gently used TVs and stereos, audiotapes, and more, more, MORE!

◆ **Use the information on the poster to answer these questions.**

1. What will be on sale at the flea market?
   - (1) clothes
   - (2) furniture and lamps
   - (3) car parts
   - (4) all of the above

2. When will the flea market take place?
   - (1) Saturday, June 21, 9:00 a.m. until 6:00 p.m.
   - (2) Saturday, May 3, 10:00 a.m. until 8:00 p.m.
   - (3) Saturday, June 20, 9:00 a.m. until 9:00 p.m.
   - (4) Saturday, March 20, 8:00 a.m. until 7:00 p.m.

3. Where will the flea market take place?
   - (1) Crabtree Theater on Route 25
   - (2) Crafters Drive-in on Route 35
   - (3) Hi-Way Drive-in Theater on Route 30
   - (4) Market Street Theater in Crabtree

4. Who will sell goods at the flea market?
   - (1) farmers from two nearby states
   - (2) artists, farmers, and dealers from three states
   - (3) dealers from the outlying suburbs
   - (4) artists and photographers from the downtown area

Did you picture in your mind the details described on the poster? For example, are you able to imagine tables full of china, glassware, and jewelry? Can you picture rows of household items and furniture? The details allow you to better understand the main idea: the Crabtree Flea Market is a sale you will not want to miss.

Here are the answers: 1. (4), 2. (3), 3. (3), and 4. (2)

Strategy: How to Find Details

- Ask the questions *Who? What? Where? When? Why?* and *How?*
- Picture in your mind what the writer describes.
- Notice how the details give you a clearer picture of the main idea.

Exercise 1

Reading directions can save your life. These directions are especially helpful because they explain why each step is important.

Read the passage and answer the questions.

Making an Emergency Kit

An emergency can happen at any time. Earthquakes, floods, and huge storms strike with little or no warning. Get ready for whatever comes your way. Make an emergency kit now.

Begin by gathering bottled water. Water is the most important thing you will need. Store at least one gallon of water for each person in your family. The water should be in plastic bottles. Avoid glass bottles because they may break.

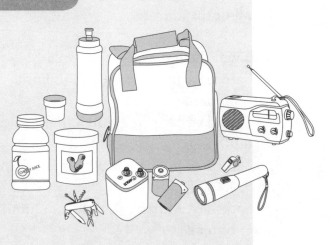

Next, stock up on food. Choose foods that do not need to be refrigerated or cooked. Examples include juice boxes, peanut butter, and granola bars. Canned meats and fruit are also good. Remember to include a can opener that can be used without electricity.

In an emergency, a family member may be injured in some way. Add a first-aid box to your emergency kit. Then you will be prepared to help if someone is hurt. Do you or other family members take any medicines regularly? If so, include a supply of these medicines in your emergency kit.

Electric power may go out, so be sure to include a flashlight. Remember to include extra batteries. Better yet, buy a flashlight that does not use batteries.

During an emergency, it is important that you can listen to the news. Emergency broadcasts will tell where to get help and how soon the danger will pass. Add a radio that runs on batteries. A whistle that you can blow to get attention is another good idea.

Put all of these items into a covered plastic box or a large backpack. Check your kit at least once a year to replace food items and batteries. You may never need this emergency kit, but it is wise to be prepared.

1. Why should you prepare an emergency kit?

_____

_____

2. List three foods that would be good to include in an emergency kit.

_____

3. Name two items that may require batteries.

_____

4. Where should you put the items you gathered for your emergency kit?

_____

5. Which sentence in paragraph 1 states the main idea of the passage?

_____

6. Which sentence in the last paragraph restates the main idea in a different way?

_____

Check your answers on page 158.

Exercise 2

Have you ever asked someone for directions and then been unable to follow the directions? Do you think that following a map is easier than following directions?

Read the passage and answer the questions.

LANGUAGE Tip

When reading a map in a mall, look first for the arrow showing where you are. Then find the shops near you. Figuring out where you are will help you find the places you are looking for.

Shopping in a Mall`

Juan Rodriguez stopped at a new shopping mall last Saturday afternoon to buy a new pair of shoes. The mall seemed enormous. In fact, it took him 15 minutes just to find a map showing where the stores were located. The mall map looked like this.

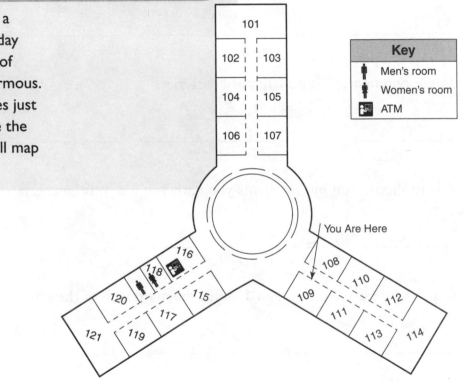

Key	
👤	Men's room
👤	Women's room
🏧	ATM

Mall Directory

101 Troutman's Department Store	108 I Scream for Ice Cream	115 Quality Sporting Goods
102 Klotz's Finer Shoes	109 Pizzarific	116 ATMs
103 Toys, Toys, and More Toys	110 Cosmetics R Us	117 Herbal Delights
104 Computer Wizard	111 Tiny Dancer Boutique	118 Public Restrooms
105 Generic Bookstore	112 Handy Hardware	119 A World of Travel
106 Hamburger Palace	113 The Piano Store	120 Mall Management Office
107 Chocolate Dreams	114 Blume's Department Store	121 Anything for a Dollar

The arrow on the map shows Juan where he is standing. There are ATMs next to the restrooms, on the way to the Anything for a Dollar store. Juan can tell from the symbols which is the men's restroom and which is the women's. If he wants to sit down, there are benches around the center of the mall. The directory tells Juan which stores match which numbers on the map.

1. Between which two stores is Juan standing as he reads the map?

   _____

2. How can Juan get from where he is standing to the toy store?

   _____

   _____

3. How will Juan find an ATM once he has left the toy store?

   _____

   _____

4. Juan's last stop is for pizza. How can he get there from the ATM area?

   _____

   _____

Check your answers on page 158.

Exercise 3

Have you ever used newspaper ads to look for an apartment? If so, you know that abbreviations can be confusing.

Read the advertisement for an apartment.

Looking for an Apartment

This is a typical ad you might read about an apartment. Most of the words are abbreviated to save space.

> Spac. apt., Lake Pk. area. 3 br, 2 ba. Conv. loc. W/D, A/C, w/w cpt., fp, balc. Utls. incl., sec. dep. req. Call John at 555-3232 eves. Avail. Oct. 1.

PART A

Match each abbreviation with the correct words.

_____ 1. br	(a) washer/dryer
_____ 2. Utls. incl.	(b) convenient location
_____ 3. A/C	(c) park
_____ 4. Conv. loc.	(d) balcony
_____ 5. sec. dep. req.	(e) wall-to-wall carpeting
_____ 6. Spac. apt.	(f) utilities included
_____ 7. W/D	(g) available
_____ 8. fp	(h) security deposit required
_____ 9. balc.	(i) fireplace
_____ 10. w/w cpt.	(j) spacious apartment
_____ 11. ba.	(k) bedrooms
_____ 12. Avail.	(l) October
_____ 13. Oct.	(m) bathrooms
_____ 14. Pk.	(n) air conditioning

PART B

Match each question with the correct answer.

_____ 1. Who is advertising the apartment?

_____ 2. How many bedrooms does the apartment have?

_____ 3. Where is the apartment located?

_____ 4. When is the apartment available?

_____ 5. What number should you call to ask about the apartment?

(a) 555-3232

(b) in the Lake Park area

(c) on October 1

(d) John

(e) 3

Check your answers on page 158.

Writing Workshop

Prewriting

Make a list of things you might pack if you were going on a vacation. Decide where you will travel to. Consider the weather. Think about the activities you will be doing. Decide how many bags (or boxes, if you are packing supplies for your car) you will need. Eliminate items from your list that you do not really need or will not have room for.

Drafting

Write a paragraph that explains what you will take on your trip. Begin the paragraph with a topic sentence. Use the items in your list as the details in your paragraph.

Revising

Read your paragraph to a partner. Think about the order of your details. Do you describe clothes, then food, and finally games for the car? Or are all the items mixed up?

Editing

Some words are difficult to spell because they sound like other words. Here are two words to watch for:

    its = ownership (Its gas tank was on the left.)

    it's = it is (It's winter now in Brazil.)

Chapter 3

Time Order

You know that seven is the number *before* eight and that Tuesday comes *after* Monday. You also know the order that events occur in most people's lives. *First*, you crawl. *Then*, you walk. *Next*, you learn to ride a bike. *Finally*, you drive a car. Words such as *before*, *after*, *first*, *then*, *next*, and *finally* are clues that help you follow time order.

Time to Plant Tomatoes

To grow tomatoes, you must first buy tomato plants. Garden shops sell tomato plants when the weather gets warm. This is usually in May. Then, water the plants before you pull them out of their pots.

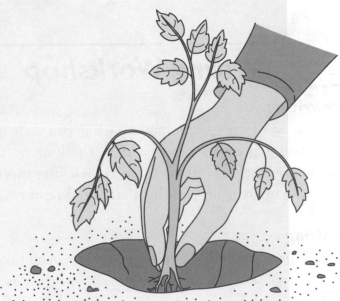

Next, dig a wide but shallow hole in the ground. Put the tomato plants in the dirt. The root system should be only four inches below the surface, where the soil temperature is still warm. All of the stem except the top couple of inches should be buried so the plant can develop strong roots.

After the plants begin to produce fruit, sprinkle fertilizer in a circle around each stem. Then water the plants well. In about a month, put at least three inches of mulch around each plant. Finally, surround the plants with wire cages. The cages will give the stems support as they start to grow. Before you know it, you will be eating juicy red tomatoes from your own garden.

◆ Look for the time-order words in the directions for growing tomatoes. Then make a list of the steps you would follow to grow tomatoes.

1. _____   5. _____

2. _____   6. _____

3. _____   7. _____

4. _____   8. _____

If your list looks like this one, you understand time order.

1. Buy tomato plants.
2. Water them.
3. Dig a hole in the ground.
4. Plant each stem.

5. Add fertilizer.
6. Water the plants.
7. Put mulch around the plants.
8. Put wire cages around the plants.

Strategy: How to Follow Time Order

- Read the entire article or set of instructions.
- Look for words such as *before, after, first, then, next,* and *finally.*
- Picture in your mind the events or the steps described.

Exercise 1

Reading directions can save you time and money. These directions provide step-by-step help for someone who wants to fix up a house but does not have much experience.

Read the passage and answer the questions.

Painting a Room

One of the quickest and least expensive ways to change the look of your home is to paint a room. However, doing a good job requires careful planning. Most of your time will be spent preparing the walls, not painting. If you follow these steps, you can have a whole new look in a room in a short time!

First, get paint samples from the hardware store. Remember that light colors make a room look bigger, while dark colors will make a room look smaller. Once you have decided on a color, measure the walls so you will know how much paint to buy.

Next, buy all the materials. You will need paint, brushes, masking tape, and drop cloths. A salesperson can help you figure out how much paint to buy. If you do not have a ladder, now may be the time to buy one. If you are painting a large area, you may want to buy a paint roller and tray.

Before you start to work on the walls, protect your furniture. If possible, move furniture out of the room. Use a drop cloth to cover furniture that cannot be moved. Put tape on window frames and other areas you do not want to paint.

The next step is to fill small holes and cracks with in the wall. Let the patches dry. Then sand the area around the spots so the walls are smooth.

Now you are ready to paint. Begin painting the edges first. Then paint across the wall, working away from the edges. When you are finished, walk out of the room and then come in again to get a fresh look at the job you have done. You may notice some spots you have missed. When you are pleased with the job you have done, it is time to clean up. Wash the paint brushes and remove the drop cloths and tape. Paint and a little hard work have given you a beautiful new room!

Listed here are the steps you need to follow to paint a room. However, the steps are not in order. Write the steps in correct order on the lines below.

clean up

1. _____

put tape where needed

2. _____

buy materials

3. _____

look for missed spots

4. _____

get paint samples

5. _____

measure the room

6. _____

paint

7. _____

cover furniture

8. _____

fill holes

9. _____

Check your answers on page 158.

Exercise 2

Do you have an automated teller machine (ATM) card from your bank? Do you prefer doing business through the machine or with a person? Do you use the ATM when the bank is closed?

Read the article. Then circle the best answer for each question.

The Automated Teller Machine

Pat Brown went to her bank to apply for an ATM card. A few days later, the bank mailed her a card that looked like a credit card. In a separate envelope, the bank mailed her a four-digit personal identification number (PIN). Pat's PIN was 1234.

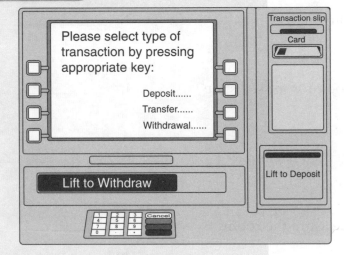

One evening Pat realized that she had only $2 in her wallet. She needed $10 the next day because she was going to a farewell lunch for a coworker. She didn't want to get up early to go to the bank, so she decided to go to the bank that night. She used her ATM card to withdraw $50 from her checking account.

These are the steps Pat followed to withdraw money. First, she put her card in the slot on the top right side of the machine. She made sure her card was facing the correct way. Second, instructions on the computer screen read, "Please enter your PIN." Pat pressed the numbers 1, 2, 3, and 4. Next, the screen read, "Please select type of transaction by pressing appropriate key." Pat pressed the key for *Withdrawal*.

Then the screen read, "From which account?" The choices it gave were *Checking, Savings,* and *Money Market*. Pat pressed the key for *Checking*. Next, the screen read, "Please select amount of transaction in multiples of ten." Pat pushed the number *5*. Then she pressed *0* three times, until the screen read "50.00." The screen then read, "Please wait." In less than a minute, it read, "Please lift the lid and remove your money."

Pat lifted the lid marked *Lift to Withdraw*. She counted her $50 to make sure the ATM had not made a mistake. Then she waited for her transaction slip to come out of the slot at the upper right corner of the machine. Pat checked the slip to make sure it was correct. Next, her ATM card was returned through the card slot. She put the card in her wallet and walked away. If Pat had made a mistake at any point by pressing the wrong button, she could have pressed *Cancel* and started over again.

1. What was Pat's first step?
   (1) pressing the withdrawal button
   (2) inserting her ATM card
   (3) counting her money
   (4) getting her transaction slip

2. What did Pat do immediately after selecting the account?
   (1) selected whether to withdraw, deposit, or transfer money
   (2) lifted the lid and removed her money
   (3) selected the amount of money she wanted to withdraw
   (4) removed her ATM card

3. When did Pat enter her PIN?
   (1) right after inserting her card
   (2) right before selecting the account
   (3) right before selecting the amount of money
   (4) right after selecting *Withdrawal*

4. When did Pat select the type of transaction?
   (1) right after selecting which account she wanted
   (2) right before receiving her withdrawal slip
   (3) right before selecting the amount
   (4) right after entering her PIN

5. What did Pat do when the screen read, "Please lift the lid . . . ?
   (1) removed her card
   (2) removed her $50
   (3) selected the type of transaction she wanted
   (4) picked up her withdrawal slip

Check your answers on page 159.

Exercise 3

Do you follow an exercise program? If so, does it include the same warm-up and cool-down phases as in the following program?

LANGUAGE Tip

aerobic   air OH bik

Aerobic comes from the word air. People do aerobic exercises so they can improve the way their bodies use oxygen.

Read the article and answer the questions.

Aerobic Exercise Session

Aerobic exercises are done to get the heart and lungs working harder. Before starting an aerobic exercise program, get your doctor's permission. The doctor will check your general physical condition and tell you whether it is safe to start exercising.

Make sure each session starts with a warm-up period. You should stretch your muscles and get them ready for your workout. Warm up for at least five minutes.

Pulse Rate	Resting Rate	Warm-Up Period 5 minutes	Aerobic Exercise 20 minutes	Cool-Down Period 5 minutes	Recovery Period
160					
150					
140					
130					
120					
110					
100					
90					
80					
70					

Then start the actual training session. Jog, bike, or do exercises that get your heart rate up to the target range. Depending on your age and your physical condition, you should try to raise your pulse rate to about 140 to 160 beats per minute. Take your pulse during exercise to make sure your heart rate does not get too fast.

After a 20-minute aerobic session, start cooling down. Do a few gentle stretches while you catch your breath. If your heart rate does not return to a resting rate (about 70) within five minutes, you are working out too hard. Finally, during the recovery period, sit down and relax.

1. How long should the aerobic exercise part of the session last?

_____

2. What comes right after the aerobic exercise?

_____

3. What should your pulse rate be at the beginning of the cool-down phase?

_____

4. How long should the warm-up phase last?

_____

5. What does the graph show as a typical resting pulse rate?

_____

Check your answers on page 159.

 ## Writing Workshop

Prewriting
List activities you do that have several steps. Next, choose one activity to write about. List the steps of the activity in logical order so they will be easy for someone else to follow.

Drafting
Write a paragraph that explains each step of your directions.

Revising
Ask a friend or a coworker to try following your directions. If any of the details are not clear, change the wording so readers will understand what they must do.

Editing
Check that every sentence and all proper nouns begin with capital letters.

UNIT 1

Review – Practical Reading

Have you ever donated blood? Have you or a member of your family ever needed blood because of an accident or an illness?

Read the article. Then circle the best answer for each question.

Giving Blood

Donating blood is a safe, easy process that can save someone's life. You can be the source of blood needed to treat people with injuries or with illnesses such as cancer, anemia, or **hemophilia.**[1] All blood types are needed at all times.

Your single donation may help three or more patients because your whole blood is broken down into parts. Each part is then used to treat a different person for a different problem. For example, red blood cells are used to treat anemia and to provide routine blood transfusions. **Platelets**[2] are used mainly for cancer patients. Fresh frozen plasma—the liquid part of the blood—is used to treat people who have clotting problems and people who are in shock.

To give blood, you must be at least 17 years old, weigh at least 110 pounds, and be in good health. It is safe to donate as often as every two months. Two months is more than enough time for your body to rebuild its supply of blood. Everyone is a potential blood recipient—someone who receives blood. Only about half of us, however, meet the age and medical requirements to be a donor—someone who gives blood. That is why it is important for everyone who can give blood to do so.

It is impossible for a donor to get AIDS—or any other illness—from donating blood if correct medical procedures are used. The blood technician should use a new sterile needle for each person who gives blood. The needle is used only once and then destroyed. Therefore, it cannot carry an infection to the next donor.

You can also give blood for a specific friend or family member who is going to have surgery. If you are scheduled for an operation, you can give blood for yourself

---

[1]**hemophilia:** an inherited blood disorder that prevents blood from clotting normally; hemophilia occurs only in males

[2]**platelets:** small disks in the blood of vertebrate animals that assist in blood clotting

ahead of time. By doing so, you can eliminate the small chance of being infected by receiving someone else's blood. All blood is screened for signs of infection before it is used. These tests are nearly 100 percent accurate. The risk from refusing a needed transfusion is far greater than the risk of infection.

It takes only an hour to give the gift of life. First, your temperature, pulse, blood pressure, and hemoglobin (iron) are checked. Your health history is reviewed. Then the nurse draws your blood. This process takes less than ten minutes. You'll give less than a pint, or one-twelfth of your blood supply.

Afterward, you will be served cookies, fruit juice, and water. Plasma is replace in about twenty-four hours, and red blood cells are replaced within four to six weeks. The process is quick and easy, and it saves lives.

1. What is the main idea of the passage?
   (1) Blood is needed constantly.
   (2) Anemia is the main reason for blood transfusions.
   (3) Donating blood is safe and easy and can save a life.
   (4) You can be the source of needed blood.

2. The blood you donate can be
   (1) broken down into parts for three or more patients
   (2) given whole to cancer patients
   (3) used only by shock victims
   (4) refrigerated for at least a year

3. You cannot give blood if you
   (1) are under 17 years old
   (2) weigh less than 110 pounds
   (3) have AIDS
   (4) all of the above

4. It is impossible to get AIDS from donating blood if correct procedures are used because
   (1) needles are used more than once
   (2) a new needle is used for each person
   (3) needles don't carry infection
   (4) needles are shared by family members only

5. When you give blood,
   (1) about a quart of liquid is removed from your body
   (2) you are asked for your health history
   (3) you cannot eat or drink anything for three hours
   (4) you will feel weak for about a month

Check your answers on page 159.

UNIT 2
Reading Nonfiction

NONFICTION includes newspaper reports, magazine articles, instructions, and books on everything from history to biography and gardening. Good reading skills can help you get a good job or learn new tasks.

To get the most out of what you read, you must do more than just recognize words. You must also be able to understand what you read. You must be able to figure out whether the writer's purpose is to inform, persuade, or entertain you. The life experience, previous knowledge, and language skills you bring to what you read will help you understand what the writer is trying to say.

Chapter	What You Will Learn About	What You Will Read
4	Main Idea and Reasons	The Mall of America Biking Is Booming What Is Closed Captioning? Do You Get Enough Sleep?
5	Facts and Opinions	Two Views on Traffic Should Pit Bulls Be Banned? Are You Vain? The Best Pizza in Town
6	Detecting Bias	Senator Robert's Campaign Speech Buy the Smooth Air Shoe! Do We Need a New Sports Park? The Franklin Sharks
7	Making Inferences	Political Campaign Cartoon Cartoons About Social Problem Cartoons About Daily Problems Arlo and Janis
Review	Reading Nonfiction	The Work of Administrative Assistants

After reading this unit, you should be able to

- find the main idea and the reasons that support that idea

- tell the difference between facts and opinions

- recognize bias and point of view

- make inferences from what you read

Chapter 4

Main Idea and Reasons

A writer often gives several reasons to support a main idea. Read this sentence:

> Sue started looking for a new job because her work was boring, it did not pay well, and her boss was a bully.

◆ The main idea is that Sue is looking for a new job. How many reasons does the writer give to support the main idea? _____

Did you write 3? The reasons are (1) her work was boring, (2) it did not pay well, and (3) her boss was a bully.

Notice how the following article about the Mall of America is organized.

LANGUAGE Tip

The first indoor mall was built in 1956 in Minnesota. Early malls were located in suburbs, far from the downtown area. Free parking soon made malls popular shopping spots.

The Mall of America

When you visit the Mall of America, wear good walking shoes. The Mall of America is the largest shopping mall in the United States. It is four stories high and covers 4.2 million square feet. No matter what you are shopping for, you should be able to find it there. The mall has more than 500 stores. The parking lot has spaces for 20,000 cars, so be sure to remember where you parked.

Even though the Mall of America is located in Minnesota, the mall is never cold. The heat from thousands of lights helps keep it warm. Some heat comes through the windows in the roof. But mostly the mall stays warm because there are always so many people inside. Even during the winter months, air conditioners keep running.

Every mall has stores. Most malls have restaurants. Many have movie theaters. The Mall of America has all these things. Of course, it has more stores, restaurants, and theaters than other malls. It is different from other malls in other ways as well. Some couples get married there. It has a wedding chapel. Some people ride a roller coaster. It has an amusement park. Others watch sharks swim. The mall even has an aquarium!

Although the Mall of America is big, there are larger malls. When Minnesota's mall opened in 1992, it was the second largest mall in the world. Since then, many other malls have been built. Today the two largest malls in the world are in China. The largest mall in North America is in Canada.

   The Mall of America, however, has more visitors than any other mall in the world. Over 40 million people go there every year. This is in addition to the 12,000 people who work in the building. Today more and more people are doing their shopping on-line. But there are still plenty of people coming to the largest shopping mall in the United States.

Let's look at how the article is organized. It has five paragraphs.
   Paragraph 1 describes where the Mall of America is and how big it is.
   Paragraph 2 explains why the air conditioning system in the mall is important.
   Paragraph 3 gives reasons why people go to the mall.
   Paragraph 4 tells why the mall is not the largest mall in the world.
   Paragraph 5 explains why some people do not go to malls.

◆ **Give a reason for using air conditioning in the Mall of America during the winter.**

You are correct if you wrote the following: **Lights, sunlight, and people heat the mall.**

◆ **Go back and underline the reasons why people go to the mall.**

You should have underlined these reasons: **stores, restaurants, movie theaters, wedding chapel, amusement park, aquarium.**

Strategy: How to Find Out Why

- Read the entire article.
- Find the main idea. What is the writer's most important point?
- Look for words such as *because, since, therefore, due to,* and *consequently.* Are they followed by reasons that tell why something has happened?
- List the reasons given in the article. Do they help you understand the main idea?

Exercise 1

How do you get to work every day? Are you ever frustrated by your method of travel and wish there were another way to get where you want to go? Would you be able to ride a bike to your job?

Read the article. Then answer each question.

Biking Is Booming

Bicycling is becoming more and more popular in the United States. It is both a sport and a way to commute to work. According to the Bicycle Institute of America, about 5 million people rode their bikes to work in 2000. Twenty years ago, only 1.5 million did. In 2002, 57 million Americans said they had ridden a bike during the summer.

Biking has become popular for many reasons. Physical fitness is perhaps the most important. "I don't have to spend an hour in the gym when I get home," says accountant Amy Packard. "I live eight miles from my job. So I get my workout by biking to and from the office."

Biking can actually be faster than driving or using public transportation. In the bike lane, Mark Simpson zips past cars in traffic jams to his job in Palo Alto, California. Riding a bike is cheaper than paying train or bus fares. It is also cheaper than paying for gas and city parking. People who are concerned about the environment like bicycles because bicycles do not pollute. In fact, some companies give away bikes to employees who promise to use them to get to work.

The safety record of bikers is also improving. The government traffic agency says this is probably due to increased use of helmets and better training of cyclists. Biking is also a great way for families to have fun together. They get fresh air and a good workout too.

There are some drawbacks to biking. The biggest one is probably bad weather. Even bike fanatics tend to stay off their wheels during the coldest, iciest months. Traffic can also be a problem. There are not enough bike paths and bike lanes on roads. For commuters, finding a safe place to park their bikes is often hard.

Chicago is one city that is trying to encourage bikers to commute to work. Within the city, there are more than 100 miles of bike lanes. All city buses have bike racks on the front of them. And bikes are allowed on trains, except during rush hours. The city's new Millennium Park, located in the downtown area, offers free parking for 300 bikes. The Cycle Center even provides lockers and showers for a small monthly fee.

1. What is the main idea of the article?
   (1) Highways are too crowded.
   (2) Bicycling is getting more popular.
   (3) Riding the bus is expensive.
   (4) You have to be a fitness nut to ride a bike.

2. What is one reason given for the increase in biking?
   (1) It is good for the rider and for the environment.
   (2) It's easy even in winter and heavy traffic.
   (3) Parking for bikes is cheap and plentiful in most cities.
   (4) Bikes are more comfortable than cars.

3. What is listed as one problem with biking?
   (1) fresh air
   (2) overdeveloped muscles
   (3) takes too long
   (4) not enough bike paths

4. Why is the safety record of bikers improving?
   (1) Smarter people are riding bikes.
   (2) Bikes are built with more advanced technology.
   (3) More riders are using helmets.
   (4) Global warming has cut down on icy weather.

5. Why do fewer people bicycle in the winter?
   (1) The weather is too cold and icy.
   (2) They are too busy watching first-run TV shows.
   (3) That is when they take vacations.
   (4) They prefer to walk then.

Check your answers on page 159.

Exercise 2

Do you ever read the words that appear on the bottom of your TV screen when people are talking? Do you know why they are there?

Read the passage and answer the questions.

LANGUAGE Tip

Sometimes closed captions are written in Spanish. They are meant to help viewers who do not speak English. However, English speakers may use the captions to learn Spanish.

What Is Closed Captioning?

When you watch a TV show or a movie, you may have seen the words that are being spoken appear in print at the bottom of the screen. This is called *closed captioning*. The words on the screen are *captions*.

Closed captioning is useful for a number of reasons. The written words are a great help for people who are deaf or hard of hearing. Many people like seeing the words so they can learn English. Written words are useful in places that are very noisy, such as airports. People who cannot hear the television are able to read the words. They also come in handy in places that must be quiet, such as hospitals.

Captioning has changed since it began in 1972. At that time, only a few programs had captions. The captioning on these shows was open—everyone saw the words whether they wanted to or not. People with hearing problems liked the captioning, but people who could hear were often annoyed. They thought the words took up too much space on the screen. This led to closed captioning. With *closed captioning*, not all viewers see the captions.

Closed captioning cannot be seen unless the TV has a special decoder. At first, people had to buy these decoders. Then they would have to attach the decoders to their TVs. However, the decoders cost a lot of money, and not many stores sold them. The government finally stepped in to help people with hearing problems. A law passed in 1990 said that all television screens 13 inches or larger had to have built-in decoders by 1993.

The captioning is added to most TV programs before the programs are aired. But for live shows, especially news programs, the captions must be written as the words are actually spoken. Someone listens carefully and types the words into a special computer program. Then the captions are added to the show. The typist must be a good speller and a fast worker.

Not all TV programs have closed captioning. However, many shows do have captions. That is good news for the people who need them. Thanks to captions, many more people are able to enjoy television.

1. What is the main idea of paragraph 2? What are three reasons given to support this idea?

   Main Idea: _____

   Reasons: _____

   _____

2. Paragraph 3 states that captioning has changed since it began in 1972. Explain how and why it has changed.

   How? _____

   Why? _____

   _____

3. Before 1993, why did deaf and hard-of-hearing people need to buy decoders for their TVs?

   _____

   _____

4. What has changed about decoders since 1993?

   _____

   _____

Check your answers on page 159.

Exercise 3

How much sleep do you get each night? Do you have trouble sleeping? How important is a good night's sleep?

Read the passage and answer the questions.

LANGUAGE Tip

Keyboarding

Notice the dashes at the end of paragraph 2. They have been placed around the definition of *insomnia*. Make a dash by typing two hyphens.

Do You Get Enough Sleep?

Americans do not get enough sleep. Experts say adults need about eight hours of sleep every night. However, most of us get far less. As many as four out of every ten Americans get fewer than seven hours.

There are a number of reasons why we do not get enough sleep. Some people have problems in their personal life or at work. Their worries keep them awake. Many stay up late watching TV. Still others would rather surf the Internet than sleep. Some go to bed but spend hours tossing and turning. These people suffer from insomnia. Insomnia—the inability to fall asleep—has become a huge problem.

Not getting enough sleep can have serious effects. Sleepy people are often grumpy and cranky. They may be unable to concentrate. Sometimes their actions make no sense. They may cry at the slightest problem or laugh wildly at the smallest joke. They may also become angry and impatient when things do not go their way. Sleepy people do not do well at work or school. They may be very bad drivers. Some people need sleep so much that they fall asleep at the wheel. Some experts think that lack of sleep is linked to road rage. Road rage (the violent behavior of drivers) can lead to accidents and fights between drivers.

Luckily, making simple changes can help many people get the sleep they need. Adults should exercise 20 to 30 minutes every morning or afternoon. They should not drink coffee or alcohol before bed. People need to turn off their TVs and computers! Going to bed and getting up at the same time every day usually helps. A regular schedule makes it easier to fall asleep quickly. Following these tips may help tired Americans sleep better.

1. What is the main idea of the article?

_____

2. Reread paragraph 2. List three reasons why many Americans get too little sleep.

_____

3. What is the main idea of paragraph 3? Give three reasons that support this idea.

Main Idea: _____

Reasons: _____

4. Why should people make the changes suggested in the last paragraph?

_____

Check your answers on page 159.

Writing Workshop

Prewriting
Make a list of activities that you enjoy. Choose one of these activities to describe to someone. Then write down reasons you enjoy the activity.

Drafting
Develop your description into a paragraph. Make sure you include the reasons why you enjoy this activity. Imagine that you are trying to persuade someone to try this activity.

Revising
Reread your paragraph to make sure that each reason is clearly explained. If one reason is more important than the others, you might introduce that reason by saying "The most important reason is . . ."

Editing
Do you have sentences that are so long they are difficult to understand? Try rewriting long sentences as two short sentences.

Chapter 5

Facts and Opinions

LANGUAGE Tip

A freeway is sometimes called an "expressway." Drivers can enter the road or leave it only at certain places. No fees are charged for driving on a freeway.

To fully understand the nonfiction that you read, you must understand the difference between facts and opinions. A **fact** can be proved by gathering information to support it. An **opinion** cannot be proved. An opinion often begins with a phrase such as *I think, I feel,* or *I believe.*

Do not believe everything you read. Letters to the editor, political speeches, and book and movie reviews are all written to persuade readers to accept the writer's opinion.

◆ **Read each of these statements. Are they** *facts* **or** *opinions*?

(1) U.S. workers are not smart enough to compete with the Japanese.
(2) Americans buy more goods from Japan than the Japanese buy from the U.S.
(3) I think that the U.S. society is healthier than the Japanese society, because the U.S. society encourages more creativity.

Only **statement 2 is a fact.** You could prove this statement by finding out how much money each country spends to buy the other country's goods.

Statements 1 and 3 are opinions. It is impossible to gather information to measure the intelligence of a large group of people. It is equally impossible to measure the health of a society on the basis of the freedom people have to create. Therefore, these statements cannot be proved.

People who write letters to the editor in newspapers and magazines may be more interested in convincing others to think as they do than in sticking to the facts. For example, read the following letters about traffic problems.

Two Views on Traffic

Let's Improve the Roads

I just read your article on how to ease traffic problems. I agree with you that we need a new freeway. I drive 20 miles to and from work every day, so I know the problem very well. The roads we have now are too crowded. There are more people moving into the area, and there are going to be more cars. I believe we should start working on the new freeway as quickly as possible. There is plenty of open land to build on. The traffic problem is bad now. Unless we start adding roads, it will get even worse.

—Morris Christensen, Chicago, Illinois

Let's Use Public Transportation

I cannot believe your solution for the traffic problem. You say we should build another freeway. I think we have too many roads right now. We do not need more roads. We need to get people to stop driving and start taking buses or trains. Aren't you tired of smelling the fumes from all those cars? And you want to make room for even more cars? Yes, the traffic is bad. But building a new freeway will not help. That just adds more cars and makes the problem worse. More homes are being built, which means we will have more people in the area. We should teach those people that it is not good to drive. It is much better to take a bus or train. Forget about building another freeway!

—Janice Wendt, Evanston, Illinois

Both letter writers read the same article. Both know that the roads have too many cars on them. But the two writers have very different ideas about how the problem should be solved. Each writer chose facts that would make his or her opinion sound like the right solution.

◆ Read the following four statements. Which are facts and which are opinions?

- I drive 20 miles to and from work every day.
- I believe we should start working on the new freeway as quickly as possible.
- I think we have too many roads right now.
- More homes are being built.

The first and fourth sentences state facts. The second and third statements are opinions. They begin with the words "I believe" and "I think." Not everyone would agree with these ideas.

Strategy: How to Tell Facts from Opinions

- For each statement, ask yourself, "Can this be proved true?"
- Watch for phrases such as *in my opinion, I think, I feel,* and *should be.* They signal that an opinion is being stated.
- Look for emotionally loaded words such as *terrible, fantastic,* and *wonderful.* These words are often used to express opinions.

Exercise 1

If you have a dog, you are probably a dog lover. However, if you have ever been bitten by a dog, you may not feel friendly toward dogs. How do these writers feel?

Read the two passages and answer the questions.

Should Pit Bulls Be Banned?

Pit Bulls Are Dangerous!

Pit bulls are vicious dogs that should definitely be banned! They were bred to take part in dogfights. Their purpose in life is to hurt other living things. Because they have been bred to fight, their jaws are extremely strong. Once a pit bull has bitten something (or someone!), it is very difficult to pry the dog's jaws open. The Centers for Disease Control have collected information about deaths caused by dog bites. Pit bulls are to blame in more than one-third of all these deaths.

The actions of a pit bull cannot be predicted. These dogs are hard to control and cannot be trusted. A quiet pit bull may suddenly attack someone for no reason. These animals are very dangerous! They should not be allowed to be kept as pets. Ban pit bulls and keep the public safe!

* * * * * * * * *

I Love Pit Bulls!

It makes no sense to ban pit bulls. Any dog can be vicious, even a small dog. How a dog behaves depends on how it is raised and trained. Most pit bulls are well-trained and very tame. It would be ridiculous to ban all pit bulls because a few are violent. Pit bulls have gotten a bad reputation that they do not deserve. Some people call any biting dog a pit bull. Often they are wrong.

Pit bulls are loved for their loyalty, bravery, and intelligence. They are some of the friendliest dogs that have ever lived. One famous pit bull is Petey. He belonged to the Little Rascals, characters in the *Our Gang* movies that were popular from the 1920s through the 1940s. Would the parents of the Little Rascals have let their children spend time with a vicious animal day after day? Of course not.

Pit bulls are no more dangerous than any other dog. Banning them is nonsense.

Write F if the statement is a fact, O if it is an opinion.

1. _____ A pit bull's purpose in life is to hurt other living things.

2. _____ Pit bulls have been bred to take part in dogfights.

3. _____ Most pit bulls are well-trained and very tame.

4. _____ Pit bulls are very dangerous!

5. _____ The Centers for Disease Control have collected information about deaths caused by dog bites.

6. _____ One famous pit bull is Petey, the Little Rascals' dog.

7. _____ Pit bulls are some of the friendliest dogs that have ever lived.

8. _____ The jaws of pit bulls are very strong.

9. _____ Banning pit bulls is nonsense.

10. _____ Pit bulls have gotten a bad reputation they do not deserve.

Check your answers on page 159.

Exercise 2

Do you read license plates as you ride down the road? Sometimes the letters and numbers on a license plate are actually messages.

Read the passage and answer the questions.

LANGUAGE Tip

Vain means "very proud of how you look." Many cars have small mirrors for the front-seat passenger to use. These are called "vanity mirrors."

Are You Vain?

Every state requires car owners to purchase license plates so their cars can be identified. When you get license plates for your car, you have a choice. Most people take whatever license plate the state gives them. About 9 million people in the country, however, want their plates to be special. They choose the letters and numbers for their plates. Usually these letters and numbers form a name or a phrase. These plates are called *vanity plates*. Car owners pay an extra fee to get these plates.

Some people think that the people who order vanity plates have high opinions of themselves. They want special license plates so everyone will notice their cars. They want people to know they are special. Other people think that these plates are silly. They say the plates are a waste of money. I do not agree with either group. I really like vanity plates.

I think it is good that people want something personal on their cars. Often people use the plates to tell little stories about themselves. By reading license numbers, you can learn something about the people who are driving near you. For example, the driver with a license plate that says I LUV MOM must be a nice person. Don't you agree?

At most, only eight numbers or letters fit on a plate. Therefore, people become creative, making up new ways to write words. L8 4 WRK stands for LATE FOR WORK.

Many drivers who don't buy vanity plates enjoy reading the messages on these plates. People who have vanity plates make driving a little more fun for everyone. PL8S R GR8!

1. Which statement is a fact?
   (1) People with vanity plates want others to know they are special.
   (2) Vanity plates are silly.
   (3) About 9 million people in this country have vanity plates.

2. Which statement is an opinion?
   (1) Vanity plates are a waste of money.
   (2) Car owners pay extra to get vanity plates.
   (3) At most, only eight numbers or letters fit on a license plate.

3. Which statement is a fact?
   (1) People who have vanity plates make driving a little more fun for everyone.
   (2) People who have vanity plates have high opinions of themselves.
   (3) Most drivers do not have vanity plates.

4. Which statement is an opinion?
   (1) People think up new ways to spell words on vanity plates.
   (2) Reading the messages on license plates is fun.
   (3) License plates have numbers and letters on them.

5. What does "PL8S R GR8" mean?

   _____

6. What message would you put on a vanity license plate?

   _____

Check your answers on page 160.

Exercise 3

LANGUAGE Tip

buffet   buh FAY

A buffet is a meal where people help themselves to a large variety of choices. Be careful—people usually eat too much when they go to buffets!

Do you have a favorite pizza restaurant? What is so special about its pizza?

Read the passage. Then answer each question.

The Best Pizza in Town

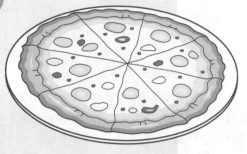

There are so many pizza places in town that it may be hard for a family to agree on where to go. I have made it my job to check out each and every pizza restaurant. I know where you can find the best meal.

Darla's Pizza is on Springtown Road, just north of the freeway. Darla's is not an ordinary take-out restaurant. You choose the food you want from a long table set up in the middle of the dining room. This fantastic buffet begins with a colorful salad bar full of healthy choices. You may be tempted to fill up on the fresh lettuce and vegetables, but save space for the main event—Darla's tasty pizza. Pizzas covered with sausage and pepperoni sit next to pizzas full of ham and pineapple.

There are plenty of non-meat pizzas too. Try the mushroom, green pepper, and spinach pizza. Or stick with a slice of pizza topped with homemade tomato sauce and oozing with cheese. There are always pizzas being baked in large brick ovens, so you know your pizza will be hot. You can't go wrong at Darla's—every pizza there is delicious!

But your meal is far from over! At the end of the buffet are Darla's out-of-this-world dessert pizzas. These can be simple thin-crust pies with sugar and cinnamon. Other dessert pizzas are covered with sliced strawberries or bananas or apples. Some customers come just for Darla's Special. That is a fabulous dessert pizza spread with creamy peanut butter and chocolate frosting. It is topped with whipped cream.

Come hungry, because you can eat all you want for one price at Darla's Pizza. You will want to return again and again.

1. Which statement is a fact?
   (1) Darla's Pizza is on Springtown Road.
   (2) Darla's has out-of-this-world dessert pizzas.
   (3) Everything in Darla's is delicious!
   (4) You will want to return again and again to Darla's.

2. Which statement is an opinion?
   (1) There are many pizza places in town.
   (2) You can eat all you want for one price at Darla's.
   (3) Darla's Special is a fabulous dessert.
   (4) There are non-meat pizzas at Darla's.

3. Which statement is a fact?
   (1) You should come hungry to Darla's Pizza.
   (2) Some of Darla's dessert pizzas are covered with sliced fruit.
   (3) It is hard for some families to decide where to eat.
   (4) You will be tempted to fill up at the salad bar.

4. Which statement is an opinion?
   (1) Darla's Pizza is north of the freeway.
   (2) Darla's serves pizza with homemade tomato sauce.
   (3) The pizzas at Darla's are baked in brick ovens.
   (4) Darla's pizza is tasty.

Check your answers on page 160.

Writing Workshop

Prewriting
What movies have you seen recently that you have strong opinions about? Choose one movie to write about. Make a list of facts and a list of opinions about the movie.

Drafting
Use your two lists to write a review of the movie. The more facts you use to support your opinions, the more likely you are that readers will agree with your review.

Revising
Check the facts you used. Be sure each fact is correct.

Editing
Even if you use the spell-check tool on a computer, you must also carefully proofread your review. The computer cannot tell whether *to, too,* or *two* is the correct word.

Detecting Bias

A writer often wants to influence readers' opinions by slanting the facts and appealing to readers' emotions. The writer might claim, "You take your life in your hands every time you leave your house. You must stop protecting criminals and start protecting victims." A writer who discusses only one side of an issue is a biased writer. The writer's **bias** can be positive or negative.

A positive bias comes across in advertisements and commercials because advertisers have a goal. They want to persuade you to buy their products. Ads often appeal to consumers' emotions and self-esteem.

> **Buy Red Silk—the perfume that makes you feel beautiful.**
> **People who drive Leopards are exciting and adventurous.**

These advertisements do not describe the negative features of the products. They do not tell you that Red Silk could give you a rash. And they do not tell you that a Leopard costs about three years' wages and has a history of needing frequent repairs. Ad writers want you to see only the good side of their products so you will buy what they are selling.

Political speeches and editorials can also be biased. These writers choose the facts that will lead readers to share their opinions. They often use "loaded words"—words that show the writer's strong opinions. When you recognize a writer's bias, you are better able to decide whether you agree with what you are reading.

LANGUAGE Tip

Synonyms

bias   BY us

These words mean the same as *bias:*

tilt	slant
leaning	prejudice
narrow-mindedness	

Senator Robert's Campaign Speech

My fellow Americans, I am here today to tell you why you should reelect me to a fourth term in the U.S. Senate. I am sure you know that the worst problem facing our country today is the lack of jobs. Many companies are reducing the number of people they employ by sending work to other countries. We need to find a way to increase employment in the United States. We need to put our people back to work.

My opponent's ideas are just plain crazy. He plans to raise taxes on businesses. How blind and stupid can he be? Doesn't he know that we must reduce the cost of business so American companies will hire American employees to produce products for Americans? Isn't he smart enough to understand that our economy can improve only by increasing the number of jobs available in America?

If you are prepared to throw away our economy to foreigners, elect my opponent. But if you want America to grow stronger, march forward into the future with me.

Did you notice the bias in the following campaign speech? Is the bias positive or negative? Underline words that show whether the candidate's speech shows a positive or negative bias.

Did you underline just plain crazy, blind and stupid, isn't he smart enough, and if you are prepared to throw away our economy to foreigners?

Note that the campaign speech does not present plans or proposals for how to increase the number of jobs. Robert's purpose is to make his opponent look bad so voters will reelect him. This is a technique used by many political candidates.

Strategy: How to Recognize Bias

- Determine how many points of view are given. If the writer presents only one side of an issue, the writing is biased.
- Look carefully at statements that sound like facts. Can the statements be proved true? If not, they are opinions.
- Watch for loaded words that try to get you to respond with your emotions instead of your mind.
- Find out whether the writer is an expert on the topic.

Exercise 1

When you're watching TV, do you ignore most of the commercials? Or do ads for soft drinks or fast-food restaurants make you thirsty or hungry? Do the ads make you think, "Yeah, I'd like to eat a big, fat, chewy chocolate-chip cookie right now"?

Read the passages and answer the questions.

PART A: BUY THE SMOOTH AIR SHOE!

"Do you want to look, feel, and play basketball like a pro? It is easy. Just buy a pair of Smooth Airs, and you'll be in good company. Most professionals have chosen Smooth Airs. They give you the extra jumping power you need for those slam-dunk shots. I scored 38 points in my last game thanks to Smooth Airs. And they're so comfortable that I even wear them off the court. Smooth Airs—for the good times in your life."

1. Find three phrases from the ad that show the athlete's bias toward Smooth Airs.

    a. _____

    b. _____

    c. _____

2. According to the ad, who will you feel like if you buy Smooth Airs?

    _____

PART B: BUY THE SMOOTH AIR SHOE!

"I wouldn't be where I am today if I didn't wear Smooth Air shoes. My feet take a lot of pounding as I walk to work from the train each day. I protect them with Smooth Airs. My feet are not tired when I represent my clients in court. They feel comfortable because of the extra layer of padding built into Smooth Air shoes. If you want your feet to feel like they're walking on air, try Smooth Airs."

Answer these questions.

1. Find three phrases from the ad that show the woman's bias toward Smooth Air shoes.

   a. _____

   b. _____

   c. _____

2. What does this advertisement suggest Smooth Airs will do for you? (You may check more than one answer.)

   _____ **(1)** protect your feet on city pavement

   _____ **(2)** make you a better athlete

   _____ **(3)** help you meet men

   _____ **(4)** help you start a new fashion trend

   _____ **(5)** help you feel like a professional woman

Check your answers on page 160.

Exercise 2

You may be biased about an issue. But to be fair, you should listen to both sides of the argument. Is this writer presenting one side or all sides of the issue?

Read the passage and answer the questions.

Do We Need a New Sports Park?

Next Tuesday the voters will decide whether a new sports park should be built in our city. Everyone agrees that children need places where they can participate in sports. They need fields where they can play baseball and soccer. They need courts where they can play basketball and tennis. The plan for the proposed park provides for all these spaces. It also includes a playground. Children of all ages will love going there.

However, some critics claim the park will cost too much money. I bet these people think schools and libraries cost too much money too. Some people say there are already enough places where the children can play. I have visited some of these places. Many are dirty and filled with trash. These places are not safe for our children. Without a safe, clean park to play in, our children will get into trouble. Is saving money more important than saving our children?

None of the other towns in the area will have such a nice sports park. All the neighboring towns will wish they had a sports park like ours. The people who do not want the park must not be proud of our city. They are stick-in-the-muds who do not like change.

The sports park will be a beautiful place. There will be trees and flowers. There will be tables where you can enjoy a picnic lunch. I guess the enemies of the park prefer ugly parking lots.

Show your love for our city's children. Show your pride in your city. Show your love of nature. Vote for the sports park next week!

1. State the two points of view discussed in "Do We Need a New Sports Park?"

_____

_____

2. The writer states that people in other towns will want a sports park. Is the writer's statement a fact or an opinion? Give a reason for your answer.

_____

_____

3. What words does the writer use to describe people who do not agree with her? Write those descriptions here.

_____

_____

_____

4. Are these descriptions fair, or do they use loaded words? Explain your answer.

_____

_____

Check your answers on page 160.

Do you have a favorite sports team? Who do you like to see your team play against?

Read the passage and answer the questions.

The Franklin Sharks

This weekend all local sports fans will be focused on one game—tomorrow's face-off between the Franklin Sharks and the Appleton Rockets. The fierce competition between the two football teams has been going on for a long time. Whenever the teams play each other, whether in Franklin or in Appleton, the stadium is full of noisy fans for both sides. This game is no different. Rockets supporters are already arriving by the carload for tomorrow's game. I think the people of Franklin should try to be gracious hosts. After all, our visitors deserve our sympathy. They are going to a lot of trouble to follow a team that is going to lose.

Another reason to treat the Rockets' fans kindly is that they will be greatly outnumbered by the Sharks' fans. The people of Franklin love their team! Every game is sold out, even though the Sharks stadium is the largest stadium in the league. When you walk down the streets of Franklin, you see lots of people wearing Sharks caps and T-shirts. Everyone is proud of this team. Who wouldn't be?

There is not a weak player on the Sharks. Every player is a big, strong guy hungry to win. The team is led by the smartest, fastest quarterback in the league. He can throw a football from here to tomorrow. I would not be surprised to see the Sharks win the game by a 30-point margin. The Rockets will struggle to score at all.

Coach Russell has been with the Sharks for 12 years. He started out great and has gotten better every season. He is able to get every member of the team to play his best. The Sharks are lucky to have a coach with his talent.

The Sharks are a strong bunch of players. They play hard. They play to win. And that is what they are going to do tomorrow night.

Circle *F* if the statement is a fact. Circle *B* if the statement shows bias.

F   B   **1.** Our visitors deserve our sympathy.

F   B   **2.** There is not a weak player on the Sharks.

F   B   **3.** Coach Russell has been with the Sharks for 12 years.

F   B   **4.** Every Sharks' game is sold out.

F   B   **5.** The Sharks are led by the fastest, smartest quarterback in the league.

F   B   **6.** Everyone is proud of the Sharks.

F   B   **7.** The Sharks are lucky to have Coach Russell.

F   B   **8.** The Sharks' stadium is the largest stadium in the league.

Check your answers on page 160.

 # Writing Workshop

Prewriting

Make a list of products you use often. Choose one item to advertise. What do you like best about this product? Write a short sentence describing your bias. Here are some examples:

- Crunch-O peanut butter is the best because it contains whole peanuts.
- Rocco's Gym has so much equipment that you never have to wait long to exercise.

Drafting

Turn your sentence into a short catchy slogan. Add a few sentences describing the benefits of your product in more detail.

Revising

Does your ad make you want to run out and buy the item? If you have used dull, uninteresting words, replace them with lively, descriptive words. Delete extra words. Advertisements are usually short. Be sure every word helps catch the readers' attention.

Editing

Look carefully at the pronouns in your ad. (Pronouns are words such as *it, them, those,* and *that*.) Be sure the meaning of each pronoun is clear. If it isn't, replace the pronoun with a noun. Example:

Unclear   They are the sweetest gumdrops you'll ever eat.
Clear   Mary's Drops are the sweetest gumdrops you'll ever eat.

Chapter 7

Making Inferences

Making an **inference** means using a stated message to figure out a message that is *not* stated directly. It means reading between the lines to see what someone really means. For example, suppose your brother is moving to a new house and you ask if he wants you to help him pack. He sighs and says, "I have a lot to do. I haven't even started packing my stereo equipment yet. Just picking up the rental truck will take a couple of hours. And I have to be out of this apartment by tomorrow afternoon. But I know how busy you are. I'll manage."

Your brother's stated message is that he can manage on his own. But what can you infer from what he says and from his tone of voice? His unstated message is that he does need help. He probably hopes you will say, "I'm not that busy. I'll be right over to help you."

Making inferences is something you do almost automatically every day. How do you know what the unstated message is? It is a kind of detective work. First, you gather clues. Then, you analyze the clues to see what they mean. Finally, you test your inference against the facts given to see if it makes sense. The following paragraph shows another example of making inferences in everyday life.

Alice had been planning this picnic for days. She spent the morning frying chicken, making potato salad, and squeezing lemons for fresh lemonade. She knew how important it was to serve cool foods on a day like this. She picked up Enríque, and they drove to the beach with the air-conditioning on full blast. When they got there, they spread out a tablecloth right next to the water. "I want to work up an appetite," said Alice. She took off her sunglasses and jumped into the lake.

◆ What is the weather like on the day of Alice's picnic? What clues (stated details) in the paragraph tell you what you need to know to make the right inference?

_____

_____

Could you tell that it was **hot and sunny**? The facts—she served cool foods, turned on the air-conditioning in the car, wore sunglasses, and went for a swim—help you arrive at that conclusion.

Often the humor in cartoons comes from the unstated message. To get the joke, the reader must use the pictures and the words to make an inference.

◆ Look at the cartoon. What are two facts (not inferences) you observe?

_____

These are the facts: Two people are watching TV. The announcer says, "The following may not be suitable for younger viewers . . . Parental guidance is suggested." The woman is puzzled. The man says, "Campaign commercial."

◆ What inference can you make from the cartoon?

_____

The cartoon suggests that **political ads might have a negative effect on young children.**

Strategy: How to Make Inferences

- Gather clues from the stated message.
- Analyze the clues to figure out what they mean.
- Test your conclusion against the facts given.
- Put all the facts and details together to make an inference.

Exercise 1

These cartoons are about social problems. What are the cartoonists saying about these problems?

Study the cartoons and answer the questions.

1. Which statements are facts that you need to know before you can understand the cartoon? **You may check ✔ more than one statement.**

    _____ Diet pills help some people lose weight.
    _____ People should eat candy while dieting so they will have more energy.
    _____ Exercise helps people lose weight.
    _____ Being overweight is a health problem.
    _____ Many TV programs teach people how to diet.

2. Which information can you *infer* from the cartoon?
    (1) The woman will probably loose weight quickly because she is taking diet pills.
    (2) The woman is not serious about losing weight.
    (3) The woman should eat more diet pills and fewer pieces of candy.
    (4) The woman always eats in front of the TV.

The word *circa* means "about." It is often used before a date when the writer is not sure of the exact date. What might happen in about the year 2050?

Barbecue Circa 2050

3. Which statement best describes what is happening in the cartoon?
   (1) The man is standing out in the rain.
   (2) The umbrella is needed because the man is not using sun screen.
   (3) The sun is very hot.
   (4) The man likes cooking his food this way.

4. What is the topic (general subject) of this cartoon?
   (1) food
   (2) rain
   (3) global warming
   (4) cooking

5. Which sentence states the cartoonist's main idea?
   (1) It is too hot today to eat in the house.
   (2) In the future, people will have to protect themselves from the sun.
   (3) One hundred years ago people cooked on open fires.
   (4) Meat tastes best when it is cooked outside.

Check your answers on page 160.

What are the cartoonists telling you about these people and their problems?

Study the cartoons and answer the questions.

Fear of news

1. What time of day is it? _____

2. Where is the woman? _____

3. What is she doing? _____

4. What are the "big, giant headlines" that the woman is referring to?

_____

_____

5. What is good about a day when the headlines are not big?

_____

_____

"Ms. Johnson, would you mind ordering me another computer? And you can cancel that call to tech-support."

6. Who is Ms. Johnson? _____

7. What had the man asked Ms. Johnson to do earlier in the day?

_____

8. What has the man just done?

_____

9. Why do you think the man solved his problem in this way?

_____

_____

Check your answers on page 160.

Exercise 3

This cartoon is about the difference in pay for men and women doing the same work. What message is the writer suggesting?

Study the cartoon and complete the exercise.

ARLO & JANIS® by Jimmy Johnson

© Newspaper Enterprise Association, Inc.

Circle S for stated fact or I for inference.

S   I   1. Janis admires the salad Arlo made.

S   I   2. Janis does not really believe that all men are great cooks even though she says she agrees with Arlo.

S   I   3. Arlo is proud of his salad-making ability.

S   I   4. The child wants to know the difference between a cook and a chef.

S   I   5. The point of the cartoon is that men and women should get equal pay for equal work.

S   I   6. Arlo believes that all the great chefs are men.

S   I   7. Arlo has a lot of self-confidence.

S   I   8. The child has been listening to the adults' conversation.

Check your answers on page 161.

Writing Workshop

Prewriting

In this chapter, you looked at several cartoons. To understand a cartoon, gather clues first by looking at the drawing. Then read the title and the words being spoken by people in the cartoon. These clues help you figure out what the cartoonist's message is.

Do you have a point you would like to get across through words and images? Make a list of subjects you feel strongly about. From the list you made, choose one situation to draw a cartoon about. Don't worry about being an artist. You can draw stick figures or cut out pictures from magazines. What the cartoon says is most important. You might create a cartoon about

- a humorous family incident or vacation
- an embarrassing situation
- en event that did not turn out the way you had planned
- a funny comment a child made to you
- a sports scene
- a dinner date that turned into a disaster
- a teacher who learned an important lesson

Drafting

Develop the situation into a cartoon. Include enough facts so your readers will have information about the issue. Don't tell them everything the characters think and feel.

Revising

Ask several people to look at your cartoon. Did they all make the inferences you intended? Ask your readers what facts they used to make their inferences. If your readers do not understand the main point you want to make, add another fact, change the words that the characters are speaking, or put more information in the title.

Editing

Check each sentence to be sure the subject and verb agree. If the subject is singular, the verb must be singular. If the subject if plural, the verb must be plural. Examples:

Singular	**Bert washes** the car every Saturday.
Plural	My **kids wash** the car after they use it.

Review—Reading Nonfiction

Have you ever felt a lot of stress at work, at home, or in school? How do you handle stress?

Read the article. Then circle the best answer for each question.

The Work of Administrative Assistants

Did you know that working women as a group have no higher rate of heart disease than homemakers? But women employed as administrative assistants do. Their heart disease rate is twice that of other women, says a medical study. This is a real problem, since millions of women work as administrative assistants. Doctors have found that the women at greatest risk either have trouble letting their anger show or have bosses who are not understanding. Many of these women have several children. Often their husbands work long hours and do not help much at home.

Why are administrative assistants more likely to have heart problems? They are often under more stress than women who are managers. Administrative assistants have a lot of responsibility. However, they do no get to make many of their own decisions. They usually have heavy work loads and tight deadlines. Yet they do often not get much appreciation for their work. And after a busy day at the office, they are expected to go home and cook, clean, and take care of their family's needs. One doctor says, "The evidence is clear. Having to please too many people and not having control over your life is bad for your health."

The situation is getting worse instead of better. Most administrative assistants today use computers on the job. Computers have made businesses more **productive**.Bosses expect that more work can be done in the same amount of time. But while productivity has gone up, pay has not always increased. Bosses often see these jobs as lower-paying positions.

---

productive: bringing more results

Computers have made administrative assistants more isolated from their coworkers. Working alone takes away one main stress reliever—complaining about the job. In addition, working at a computer screen all day adds to the stress. Workers may be concerned about eye strain. They may have physical pain because of the repeated hand movements done to move the mouse and enter data. They may watch as the computer counts their keystrokes or measures how much work has been done.

Increased stress equals greater risk of heart disease. Some of the solutions are simple. Administrative assistants should make an effort to get exercise, eat right, and learn to relax. But other solutions are harder to reach. More businesses must learn to value the work that administrative assistants do.

1. Which women have the greatest risk of having heart attacks?
   (1) those who are managers
   (2) those who cannot express anger or who have bosses who are not understanding
   (3) those who use computers
   (4) those who get exercise and eat right

2. Which of the following statements is a fact?
   (1) Everyone thinks computers are wonderful.
   (2) Most businesses have learned to value administrative assistants.
   (3) Families provide more stress than relaxation.
   (4) Administrative assistants have a higher rate of heart disease than homemakers.

3. Which of the following statements is an opinion?
   (1) Administrative assistants have twice as much risk of having heart attacks as other women do.
   (2) Computers have increased office productivity.
   (3) Administrative assistants like having lots of responsibility.
   (4) Computers can count keystrokes and measure how much work is done.

4. The writer's bias is
   (1) in favor of bosses
   (2) against men
   (3) against work
   (4) in favor of administrative assistants

Check your answers on page 160.

UNIT 3
Reading Poetry

POETRY might not seem very important. After all, it does not usually tell you how to do something or describe what is happening in the news. But what poetry does better than any other kind of writing is capture feelings in words.

You may not read poetry very often, but poetry does touch your life. If you listen to songs—from blues to pop, from rap to rock—you're listening to poetry. As you read the poems in this unit, try to hear them the way you hear a song.

Chapter	What You Will Learn About	What You Will Read
8	Form	"Concrete Cat" "Well, Yes" "We Real Cool" "A Seeing Poem"
9	Rhythm and Rhyme	Two Limericks "Eldorado" "Steam Shovel" "Daddy Fell into the Pond"
10	Imagery	"Dust of Snow" "The Desert" "First Lullaby" "If Love Had Wings"
11	Similes and Metaphors	"The Road Not Taken" "Mother to Son" "Apartment House" "Grandpa"
Review	Reading Poetry	"Joe"

After reading this unit, you should be able to

- identify the form of a poem
- identify rhythm and rhyme
- identify imagery
- recognize similes and metaphors

Chapter 8

Form

One of the first things you notice when you read a poem is the poem's **form**. Form includes the number of lines in each **stanza**, or verse, and the length of each line. Form is the way a poem looks on the page. For example, this poem is written in two stanzas.

Fog

The fog comes
on little cat feet.

It sits looking
over harbor and city
on silent haunches
and then moves on.

—Carl Sandburg

LANGUAGE Tip

Multiple Meanings

In this lesson, *concrete* means "true-to-life" or "realistic." *Concrete* can also mean "a material made from cement, sand, gravel, and water."

How long the lines are and where the lines break may have nothing to do with where the sentences end. Instead, the lines are clues to help you understand the feelings and the meaning that the poet wants to get across. Notice the space between the two verses of the poem "Fog." You should pause when there is extra space between words or lines.

Many poems are written in **free form**. These poems do not follow a set pattern. Sometimes poets play with the placement of words. The shape of the poem may look like the object that the poem is about. These poems are called **concrete poems**. The following poem is a good example of a poem with a shape.

Concrete Cat

— Dorthi Charles

Did the meaning of this poem hit you before you read the poem? Did you see the shape of the cat as you read the words? If so, the poem succeeded.

◆ **Answer the questions in the space provided.**

Why did the poet capitalize the *A* in *ear* and the *U* in the *mouth*?

_____

The capital letters show the **pointed shape of the ears** and the **rounded shape of the mouth.**

What words in the poem are not parts of the cat?

_____

The words **dish, litterbox,** and **mouse.**

What sense (touch, sound, sight, smell, or taste) does this poem appeal to?

_____

It appeals to the sense of **sight.**

Strategy: Understanding Form

- Before reading a poem, notice how the poem looks.
- Is the poem broken into stanzas, or verses? Notice that each verse is probably about a different idea.
- Do the words in the poem form the shape of an object?
- After you read a poem, think about the feeling that the poem gives you. Does the form of the poem add to that feeling?

Exercise 1

Do you like candy bars? What is your favorite candy bar? What ingredients are in your favorite candy bar? Does this poem make you hungry for a candy bar?

Read the poem. Then circle the best answer for each question.

Well, Yes
Candy bar—

```
    co \ a t e c h o c o l a t e c h o            c
  c                                                  o
    o      pea-    pea-   pea-    pea-                \
  o       pea-  nuts   nuts    nuts    pea-         a
           nuts                          nuts    pea-   t
  h    pea-                                      nuts     e
         nuts      r s h m a l                            a
  c                m                   l                  t
         pea-     m           caramel caramel caramel  o  e
  c      nuts      a                             w   pea-  t
  h                 r s h m a l                  w   nuts   a
  o      pea-               l  l                           \
         nuts  pea-                     pea-   pea-     o
  c            nuts   pea-  pea-  pea-  nuts   nuts   c
    o                 nuts  nuts  nuts                  o
      \ a t e c h o c o l a t e c h o              c
```

Too much.
Too much.
But I'll have one more.

— by Robert Froman

1. In what way does the arrangement of the words in the poem look like a candy bar?
    (1) The word *chocolate* is printed over and over again in the rectangular shape of a candy bar.
    (2) The words are layered like the parts of a candy bar.
    (3) The chocolate is on the outside, and the other ingredients are on the inside.
    (4) all of the above

2. Which senses does this poem appeal to?
    (1) sight and taste
    (2) sight and smell
    (3) smell and hearing
    (4) touch and taste

3. What do the last three lines of the poem mean?
    (1) The speaker had too many candy bars.
    (2) The speaker feels full but will have another candy bar.
    (3) The speaker will not eat any more candy bars.
    (4) The speaker does not like to eat candy bars.

4. Which four ingredients does the candy bar in the poem contain?
    (1) peanut butter, marshmallow, chocolate, raisins
    (2) peanuts, chocolate, coconut, marshmallow
    (3) chocolate, almonds, marshmallow, peanuts
    (4) chocolate, peanuts, caramel, marshmallow

5. Which candy bar is most like the candy bar in the poem?
    (1) Hershey Bar
    (2) Butterfinger
    (3) Snickers
    (4) PayDays

Check your answers on page 161.

Exercise 2

This poem does not have the shape of an object. But its form is important to its meaning. What is unusual about the form of this poem?

Read the poem and answer the questions.

LANGUAGE Tip

Gwendolyn Brooks (1917–2000) was an African American writer. She lived most of her life in Chicago. Brooks often wrote about the African American community.

We Real Cool

The Pool Players.
Seven at the Golden Shovel.

    We real cool. We
    Left school. We

5   Lurk late. We
    Strike straight. We

    Sing sin. We
    Thin gin. We

    Jazz June. We
10 Die soon.

       —Gwendolyn Brooks

1. How many people are playing pool? _____

2. What is the name of the pool hall? _____

3. How many stanzas are in this poem? _____

4. How many lines are in each stanza? _____

5. The poet ends almost every line with the word "We." Why do you think she placed that word at the end of the line instead of at the beginning of the next line?

_____

_____

6. Readers can picture the speaker of this poem even though he is not described. Describe how you imagine the speaker in this poem looks, sounds, and acts.

_____

_____

_____

7. Which word best describes the pool players? Circle the word and explain why you chose it.

    proud   angry   funny   happy-go-lucky   worried

_____

_____

Check your answers on page 161.

Exercise 3

What does the shape of this poem remind you of? Does it turn on a light in your mind?

Read the poem. Then circle the best answer for each question.

A Seeing Poem

– Robert Froman

1. Why did the poet use all capital letters in the poem?
   (1) to show that all letters in the poem have the same importance
   (2) to show that all words in the poem have the same importance
   (3) because he likes capital letters better than small letters
   (4) because he wants the words to create a smooth shape

2. What sense does this poem appeal to most?

(1) smell

(2) hearing

(3) sight

(4) taste

3. What do you think was the poet's main purpose for writing this poem?

(1) to surprise and entertain readers

(2) to persuade readers to buy light bulbs

(3) to inspire readers to create their own poems

(4) to describe why poems should have concrete shapes

Check your answers on page 161.

Writing Workshop

Prewriting

The words in a concrete poem form the shape of the object they are describing. Make a list of objects you could write a concrete poem about.

Choose one object from your list. Then make a list of words or phrases that describe the object. For example, these words could be used to describe a cloud: *fluffy, white, high, soft, airy, constantly moving.*

Drafting

Now that you have chosen an object and listed the details you want to include, write a poem. Then write the words so they form the shape of the object you are describing. You will have written a concrete poem.

Revising

With a partner, look at the shape of your poem. What does your partner understand about your topic before reading the poem? Do any words need to be moved? Should any words be written larger, bolder, or with capital letters?

Editing

Read the words of the poem carefully. Look at the punctuation. Think about whether dashes or commas would help the reader understand the words.

Chapter 9

Rhythm and Rhyme

Before people wrote stories, they told stories. Rhythm and rhyme helped them remember the stories.

Rhythm is all around us. Your heart beats in a steady rhythm. You walk with a certain rhythm. If you are in the habit of tapping a pencil when you are thinking, you tap in a rhythm.

If you stop wherever you are and listen, you will probably hear a rhythm. It might be the song of a bird, the tick of a clock, or the clackety-clack of a subway train. And, of course, the music you listen to has a rhythm.

Poets create rhythm in different ways. Rhythm may come from the number of syllables in a line or from the repeating of words. It may come from the echo of certain sounds. For example, in "*Peter Piper p*icked a *p*eck of *p*ickled *p*eppers," the rhythm is created by the *p* sound at the beginning of most words.

Poets also create rhythm by using words that rhyme, either at the end of lines or within lines. When we say two words **rhyme**, we mean that the ends of words sound alike. For example, "the *moon* in *June*" is a rhyme. So is "the *cat* in the *hat*." Poems with rhyme usually have rhyme patterns. Here is an example of a poem with a rhyme pattern.

> I eat my peas with honey.
> I've done it all my life.
> They do taste kind of funny,
> But it keeps them on the knife.

The rhyme pattern in this poem is very common. The first line rhymes with the third line, and the second line rhymes with the fourth line.

Limericks are humorous poems that always follow the same rhyme pattern. The first, second, and fifth lines rhyme, and the third and fourth lines rhyme. The writers of most limericks are **anonymous**, or unknown. Look at the two limericks that follow.

Two Limericks

There was a young lady of **Lynn**[1]	A boy who weighed many an **oz**.[3]
Who was so uncommonly thin	Used language I will not pronoz.
That when she **essayed**[2]	His sister one day
To drink lemonade	Pulled his chair right away.
She slipped through the straw and fell in.	She wanted to see if he'd boz.

[1]**Lynn:** a city in Massachusetts
[2]**essayed:** tried
[3]**oz.:** ounce (1/16 of a pound)

◆ Answer these questions about the rhymes in the two limericks.

In the first limerick, which words rhyme? _____ _____

In the first limerick, *Lynn, thin,* and *in* rhyme. *Essayed* and *lemonade* also rhyme.

In the second limerick, which words rhyme? _____

The second limerick is a bit tricky. In the first line, the word *ounce* is abbreviated as *oz*. Then the poet has fun by abbreviating the words that rhyme with *ounce*—*pronounce* and *bounce*. In this limerick, *oz., pronoz.,* and *boz.* rhyme. *Day* and *away* also rhyme.

Both limericks have the same rhyme pattern. They also have the same rhythm. Notice that lines 1, 2, and 5 are long and that lines 3 and 4 are short.

Strategy: How to Identify Rhythm and Rhyme

- As you read a poem aloud, listen for the beat. The beat is the poem's rhythm.
- Look for words that are repeated.
- Listen for words that start with the same sound.
- Listen for rhymes. Does the last word of one line sound like the last word of another line?
- Look for rhyming words within lines too.

Exercise 1

What has the knight in this poem spent his life doing?

Read the poem and complete the exercise.

LANGUAGE Tip

El dorado means "the man covered with gold" in Spanish. Eldorado is often used to mean "a place where everyone is rich." People look for Eldorado when they are never satisfied with what they have.

Eldorado

Gaily **bedight**,[1]
A gallant knight
In sunshine and in shadow,
Had journeyed long,
5   Singing a song,
In search of Eldorado.

But he grew old—
This knight so bold—
And o'er his heart a shadow
10   Fell as he found
No spot of ground
That looked like Eldorado.

And, as his strength
Failed him at length,
15   He met a pilgrim **shadow**[2]—
"Shadow," said he,
"Where can it be—
This land of Eldorado?"

"Over the Mountains
20   Of the Moon,
Down the Valley of the Shadow,
Ride, boldly ride,"
The **shade**[3] replied—
"If you seek for Eldorado!"
                    —Edgar Allan Poe

---

[1] **bedight:** clothed
[2] **shadow:** ghost *or* spirit
[3] **shade:** another word for *shadow*

Circle *T* if the statement is true or *F* if it is false.

T   F   **1.** The knight in the poem is a young man.

T   F   **2.** The lines in the poem are all about the same length.

T   F   **3.** Each line ends with a period, a comma, or a dash.

T   F   **4.** Lines 1 and 2 in each verse rhyme.

T   F   **5.** Lines 3 and 6 and lines 4 and 5 rhyme in each verse.

T   F   **6.** The words *Mountains* and *Moon* (lines 19 and 20) rhyme.

T   F   **7.** The pilgrim tells the knight to keep riding if he wants to find Eldorado.

T   F   **8.** Repeating the word *Eldorado* in the last line of each verse helps create the rhythm in the poem.

Using words that begin with the same sound helps create rhythm in the poem. Next to each word, write a word beginning with the same sound that appears near this word in the poem.

9. gaily _____

10. singing _____

11. fell _____

12. looked _____

Circle the best answer for the question.

13. Line 3 means that the knight looked for Eldorado
    (1) when he was young and old
    (2) whether there was sunshine or clouds
    (3) far and near
    (4) when he was rich and poor

14. Which sentence best states the main idea of the poem?
    (1) The knight lived in the land of gold for many years.
    (2) The knight is sure he will soon come to Eldorado.
    (3) The knight has been looking for the land of gold but has not found it.
    (4) The knight meets a good friend as he travels to Eldorado.

Check your answers on page 162.

A steam shovel is a large shovel powered by a steam engine. It was used for moving large amounts of dirt. According to the speaker in this poem, a steam shovel looked like a prehistoric animal.

LANGUAGE Tip

Steam shovels were invented in 1839. To dig the Panama Canal, 102 steam shovels worked from 1904 through 1914.

Read the passage and answer the questions.

Steam Shovel

The dinosaurs are not all dead.
I saw one raise its iron head
To watch me walking down the road
Beyond our house today.
5 Its jaws were dripping with a load
Of earth and grass that it had **cropped**.[1]
It must have heard me where I stopped,
Snorted[2] with steam my way,
And stretched its long neck out to see,
10 And chewed, and grinned quite **amiably**.[3]

—Charles Malam

---

[1]**cropped:** cut off the top layer
[2]**snorted:** made a loud noise by blowing air through one's nose
[3]**amiably:** friendly

Circle *T* if the statement is true or *F* if it is false.

T   F   1. The speaker thinks steam shovels look like dinosaurs.
T   F   2. The words at the end of lines 1 and 3 rhyme.
T   F   3. The words at the end of lines 4 and 8 rhyme.
T   F   4. The lines in the poem are all about the same length.
T   F   5. In the beginning of the poem, the speaker seems to be afraid of the steam shovel.

Answer these questions.

6. Which pair of words does NOT rhyme?
   (1)   dead / head
   (2)   road / load
   (3)   today / see
   (4)   cropped / stopped

7. In line 2, what is the iron head?

_____

_____

8. Why is the steam shovel described as having jaws (line 5)?

_____

_____

9. Explain what the steam shovel is doing when it "stretched its long neck."

_____

_____

Check your answers on page 162.

Exercise 3

LANGUAGE Tip

This poem has an unexpected rhyme. Look at the two lines written in capital letters. Alfred Noyes was having fun when he wrote this poem!

This is a funny poem about an event that happened on a very gloomy day. What would you do if you saw this happen? Would this event cheer you up?

Read the poem. Then answer each question.

Daddy Fell into the Pond

Everyone grumbled. The sky was gray.
We had nothing to do and nothing to say.
We were nearing the end of a **dismal**[1] day,
And there seemed to be nothing beyond,
5   THEN
Daddy fell into the pond!

And everyone's face grew merry and bright,
And Timothy danced for sheer delight,
"Give me the camera, quick, oh quick!"
10   He's crawling out of the duckweed." Click!

Then the gardener suddenly slapped his knee,
And doubled up, shaking silently,
And the ducks all quacked as if they were **daft**[2]
And it sounded as if the old drake laughed.

15   O, there wasn't a thing that didn't respond
                  WHEN
Daddy fell into the pond!

—Alfred Noyes

---

[1]**dismal:** sad, gloomy
[2]**daft:** crazy

1.   Which lines in verse 1 rhyme? _____

2. How does the feeling in this poem change? _____

3. Why might the poet have set the words *THEN* and *WHEN* on lines by themselves?

_____

4. What is the rhyme pattern in this poem? _____

5. What does "Then the gardener suddenly slapped his knee" (line 11) mean?

_____

Check your answers on page 162.

 ## Writing Workshop

Prewriting
Make a list of activities you like to do. Then choose one activity as the topic of a poem. Think of words that rhyme with your topic. For example, *zoo* rhymes with *new, do,* and *true.* Then list words that rhyme with key words you might use in your poem. *Bird* rhymes with *third, word, blurred,* and *heard.*

Drafting
As you write a poem, use rhyming words at the end of lines.

Revising
Look back through the poems you've already read and notice their different rhyme patterns. Be sure the rhymes in your poem have a pattern.

Editing
Poets often use a capital letter at the beginning of each line, even if the first word in that line is not the beginning of a new sentence. Check for capital letters in your poem.

Chapter 10

Imagery

Poets use words the way artists use paints. Words help poets create pictures, or images, in the minds of their readers. When a poet uses words to describe something so clearly that the reader can see it, the poet is using **imagery**.

Sight is not the only sense that poets use. They may also describe their world in terms that help readers hear, taste, smell, and touch something. Poets try to appeal to all five senses.

Imagine walking down a city street in the summertime. Can you feel the muggy air on your skin? Can you taste the grit in the air from too much traffic? Can you smell hot dogs or other foods? What words would you use to describe your city to someone who has never been there?

Poets choose their words carefully. They may use images to bring scenes to life. They want their words to give readers a better understanding of life. Poems have many ways of helping us see more clearly.

The poem "Dust of Snow" captures an image and then uses the image to make a point. The second verse describes how the speaker feels when looking at the image.

Dust of Snow

The way a crow
Shook down on me
The dust of snow
From a **hemlock**[1] tree

5 Has given my heart
A change of mood
And saved some part
Of a day I had **rued**.[2]

—Robert Frost

---

[1]**hemlock:** an evergreen tree
[2]**rued:** regretted

◆ What image does Robert Frost want you to <u>see</u> in your mind's eye?

_____

_____

You have a good idea of the picture Frost was describing if you wrote **a crow landing in an evergreen tree and then shaking some snow from the branches.**

◆ What other senses do you experience as you read this poem?

_____

You might experience the sense of **touch.** You can image feeling cold as the wet snow falls on you.

◆ In the second verse, the speaker uses the same image to make a point about life. He says the falling snow has given his heart a change of mood. Do you think it has made him happier or sadder?

_____

It has made him **happier.** Frost is suggesting that some small event can cheer you up no matter how big your problems seem. Seeing this one example of nature's beauty has turned the speaker's whole day around.

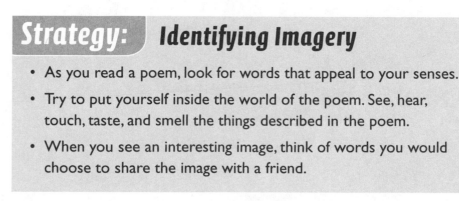

Strategy: *Identifying Imagery*

• As you read a poem, look for words that appeal to your senses.

• Try to put yourself inside the world of the poem. See, hear, touch, taste, and smell the things described in the poem.

• When you see an interesting image, think of words you would choose to share the image with a friend.

Exercise 1

When you walk, do you see, hear, and feel the things around you as this young Native American man does?

Read the poem and answer the questions.

The Desert

As I walk in the desert
I see a coral snake passing by,
and the bright sun shines the day.

I hear birds singing on a
5 mesquite tree. I hear animals
crying for food and water.

I feel a strong breeze passing by,
and the animals come to me
so I can touch them.

10 So, next time you are in
a desert, like me, see things,
feel things, and hear things.

—Eucario Mendez

1. What sense does the speaker appeal to in verse 1? _____

2. What sense does he appeal to in verse 2? _____

3. What sense does he appeal to in verse 3? _____

4. What image does the speaker want the reader to see in verse 1?

_____

5. What does the speaker feel as he walks?

_____

6. How many verses does this poem have?

_____

7. What is the rhyme pattern in the poem?

_____

8. How does the last verse summarize the ideas in the poems?

_____

_____

Check your answers on page 162.

Exercise 2

Have you ever been at the beach in the late afternoon? This poem will help you remember the experience. The speaker is a child at the beach with his family.

Read the passage and answer the questions.

First Lullaby

In late afternoon
the sea breathes
coolness
onto the shore.

5 Lying on a towel
I feel the sand still glowing
with the memory of the day's hottest sun.

The beach hushes
at this time of day
10 and it sounds like the
world's first lullaby:
the low throaty waves,
salty breeze in my ears,
and Mom humming.

—Ralph Fletcher

1. What images in the poem appeal to the sense of touch?

_____

_____

2. What images in the poem appeal to the sense of hearing?

_____

_____

3. What does the speaker compare these sounds to?

_____

4. How many stanzas does this poem have? _____

5. What is the rhyme pattern in the poem? _____

_____

6. How do the things that are seen, heard, and touched make the speaker feel? Explain your answer.

_____

_____

_____

7. List three things you can see, hear, smell, taste, or touch that make you feel happy and peaceful.

_____

_____

Check your answers on page 162.

Exercise 3

The speaker of this poem is imagining how the world could be changed. How does the speaker think this change will happen?

Read the poem and answer the questions.

> **LANGUAGE Tip**
>
> *Homophones*
>
> Homophones are words that sound alike but are spelled differently.
>
> *Soar* means "sail in the air" or "glide."
>
> *Sore* means "painful."

If Love Had Wings

```
    If love had wings
         it would soar the sky,
    Searching for heartache
         or a lost child's cry.
 5  It would then touch down
         on this world of pain
    So each lonely person
         would know its name.
    Then once again
10        it would take to flight
    And search for hatred
         throughout the night.
    Its wings would shelter
         all the land,
15  Protecting each child,
         woman and man.
    Yes, the world would speak
         of happy things
    And live in peace,
20        if love had wings.
```

—Deborah Sanders

1. What image does the speaker use of love moving through the world?

_____

2. What images of sound does the poet use?

_____

3. Which pairs of words in the poem rhyme? (Notice that some words, such as *pain* and *name*, almost rhyme.)

_____

4. What makes you think that the speaker does not believe the world will be peaceful?

_____

_____

Check your answers on page 162.

Writing Workshop

Prewriting

Make a list of things that you see, hear, smell, taste, and feel as you walk around.

Drafting

Use these images in a poem. You may use one verse for each sense (like the poem on page 86). Or you may write a new verse for various places where you walk to.

Revising

Read your poem. Be sure each image is clear and vivid so it appeals to the senses. Now ask a friend to read your poem. Can your friend walk into the world you've described?

Editing

Check words that show comparisons and contrasts. When you compare two things in your poem, you may use adjectives that end in *er*. Example: faster. If the adjective is a long word, use the word *more* to make the comparison. Example: more beautiful.

Chapter 11

Similes and Metaphors

Poets often compare two things. When they describe an object or an idea, they often compare it to something their readers are likely to be familiar with.

A **simile** uses the word *like* or *as* to state a comparison. You may say, "The athlete moves like the wind." People know you do not mean that the athlete is invisible or that he knocks leaves off trees. You mean he is very fast.

A metaphor also compares two unlike things, but it does not use *like* or *as*. You might read, "The moon is a silver platter." You know that the moon is not a silver platter. But this metaphor helps you imagine what the moon looks like.

The first poem below contains similes. The second poem uses a metaphor.

O my love's like a red, red rose
    That's newly sprung in June;
O my love's like the melody
    That's sweetly played in tune.
        —from "A Red, Red Rose"
            by Robert Burns
	"Hope" is the thing with feathers—
	That perches in the soul.
	And sings the tune without the words—
	And never stops—at all— . . .
	    —from "'Hope' Is the Thing with Feathers"
	          by Emily Dickinson

◆ **Answer these questions about the similes and the metaphor in these poems.**

What two things does the speaker in "A Red, Red Rose" compare his lover to?

_____

The speaker compares his love to a **red rose** and a **song**. Since most people can picture roses and lovely songs, the similes help readers understand what the lover is like.

What is Hope compared to? _____

Hope is compared to a **bird.** A bird is free to fly anywhere. It sings without effort, and its song seems to go on forever.

Poets use similes and metaphors to help get across feelings and deeper meaning. They can turn an unclear idea into an image you can see and touch and, therefore, understand.

On the next page are two verses from a famous poem. The whole poem is a metaphor.

The Road Not Taken

Two roads **diverged** in a yellow wood,
And sorry I could not travel both
And be one traveler, long I stood
And looked down one as far as I could
To where it bent in the undergrowth. . . .

And both that morning equally lay
In leaves no step had trodden black.
Oh, I kept the first for another day!
Yet knowing how way leads on to way,
I doubted if I should ever come back. . . .

—Robert Frost

diverged: spread apart

◆ **Answer these questions about the poem "The Road Not Taken."**

What is the speaker thinking about when he describes the two roads? _____

What is the speaker suggesting in the last three lines?

_____

The two roads may be the many possible paths in life. The last three lines suggest that each decision you make in life moves you in a new direction.

Strategy: How to Recognize Similes and Metaphors

- Look for the word *like* or *as*.
- Look for comparisons between two unlike things.
- Picture each image in your mind.

Exercise 1

Can you remember some important advice that one of your parents gave you when you were young? Do you have words of wisdom you would like to pass on to your children or to a friend?

LANGUAGE Tip

Langston Hughes (1902–1967) lived in the Harlem neighborhood of New York City. Hughes is known for helping writers and artists celebrate black life and culture through their work.

Read the poem. Then answer the questions.

Mother to Son

Well, son, I'll tell you:
Life for me ain't been no crystal stair.
It's had tacks in it,
And splinters,
5   And boards torn up,
And places with no carpet on the floor—
Bare.
But all the time
I'se been a-climbin' on,
10 And reachin' landin's,
And turnin' corners,
And sometimes goin' in the dark
Where there ain't been no light.
So, boy, don't you turn back.
15 Don't you set down on the steps
'Cause you find it kinder hard.
Don't you fall now—
For I'se still goin', honey,
I'se still climbin',
20 And life for me ain't been no crystal stair.

—Langston Hughes

1. Which sentence sums up the meaning of this poem?
   (1) The mother wants her son to be a carpenter so the stairs are repaired.
   (2) The mother does not want her son to give up when times are hard.
   (3) The mother lives in a fifth-floor apartment.
   (4) The mother is worried that her son may be afraid of heights.

2. How do the lengths of the lines relate to the subject of the poem?
   (1) They don't.
   (2) They vary as the mother and son get closer and then farther apart.
   (3) Some lines are longer, just as some steps are harder to climb.
   (4) The lines resemble steps, showing how steps get shorter at the top.

3. What do you think the poet intended readers to see in their mind's eye when they read this poem?
   (1) the mother running up a flight of glass steps
   (2) the son relaxing on the steps, thinking about life
   (3) the mother walking up a dark, rundown stairway at the end of a long day
   (4) the place at the top of the stairs

4. Do you think the mother has had an easy life or a hard life? What words make you think so?

   _____

   _____

5. Is the mother's advice encouraging or discouraging? What makes you think so?

   _____

   _____

Check your answers on page 163.

Exercise 2

Be sure to read the title of this poem. It will help you understand the comparison that the speaker is making.

Read the passage and answer the questions.

Apartment House

A filing-cabinet of human lives
Where people swarm like bees in tunneled hives,
Each to his own cell in the towered comb,
Identical and cramped—we call it home.

—Gerald Raftery

1. Which thing is NOT compared to an apartment building in this poem?
   (1) a bee hive
   (2) a honeycomb
   (3) a subway
   (4) a filing cabinet

2. Which phrase contains a simile?
   (1) A filing cabinet of human lives
   (2) people swarm like bees
   (3) Each to his own cell in the towered comb
   (4) we call it home

3. Which of these phrases is a metaphor for an apartment house?
   (1) A filing cabinet of human lives
   (2) people swarm like bees
   (3) Identical and cramped
   (4) we call it home

4. How is an apartment house like a filing cabinet?

   _____

   _____

5. How is an apartment house like a bee hive?

   _____

   _____

6. Which pairs of words in the poem rhyme?

   _____   _____

Check your answers on page 163.

Exercise 3

What does the speaker think about his grandfather?

Read the poem and complete the exercise.

LANGUAGE Tip

Suffixes

By adding -y to the end of a noun, you can change the noun to an adjective.

Dust becomes *dusty*.

Knob (bump) becomes *knobby*.

Grandpa

His eyes glow like pearls in the water
sitting like a majestic eagle
staring into nothing—
dusty old hat
5 that's seen many years.

Knobby old cane shines in the sun;
he walks through the small
sand canyon which once was flat.
The lizard bows to the aging man
10 for soon he will be gone
like the lady he loves.

Cars zooming by like a train of ants—
the sound of kids playing
like the sound of a storm
15 he only can hear—
the thought of the years.

—Shandin Pete

Circle *T* if the statement is true or *F* if it is false.

T   F   **1.** In the first verse, Grandpa's pearls are compared to water.

T   F   **2.** The comparison in line 1 is a simile.

T   F   **3.** Grandpa is compared to an eagle because of how he flies through the village.

T   F   **4.** The comparison in line 12 is a metaphor.

T   F   **5.** Grandpa does not actively participate in village life.

T   F   **6.** Life is changing in Grandpa's village, but he does not change.

T   F   **7.** Lines 1 and 3 rhyme in each verse.

T   F   **8.** All the lines in the poem have the same rhythm.

T   F   **9.** "Cars zooming" (line 12) appeals to the sense of sight.

T   F   **10.** The images of pearls, eagles, and bowing lizards show Grandpa is respected.

Check your answers on page 163.

Writing Workshop

Prewriting

Turn these items into metaphors or similes by completing the sentences.

The bus during rush hour is like _____.

A hot shower is _____.

A spider is like _____.

Drafting

Pick a simile or metaphor from the list above. What images and feelings does it bring to mind? Write a paragraph describing the subject you chose. Include details that appeal to the senses. Then, add line breaks, rhyme, and rhythm to turn your idea into a poem.

Revising

Read your poem out loud. Does it flow? Does it paint a picture? Have you used a simile or metaphor?

Editing

If you have used contractions in your poem, be sure the apostrophe appears where letters have been omitted. Examples: don't, there's, I'll, they're.

Review—Reading Poetry

Do you like to watch birds? Do you feed birds or ducks or chipmunks? Have you ever watched animals at a zoo?

Read the poem. Then circle the best answer for each question.

Joe

We feed the birds in winter,
And outside in the snow
We have a tray of many seeds
For many birds of many breeds
5   And one gray squirrel named Joe.

But Joe comes early,
Joe comes late,
And all the birds
Must stand and wait.
10   And waiting there for Joe to go
Is pretty cold work in the snow.

—David McCord

Circle the best answer for each question.

1. What is the main idea of this poem?
   (1) The speaker feeds many kinds of birds.
   (2) The greedy squirrel eats the birds' food.
   (3) The birds need food most in the winter.
   (4) The birds do not like the squirrel.

2. Who is Joe?
   (1) the speaker
   (2) the hungriest bird
   (3) the person who feeds the birds
   (4) the squirrel

3. What can you say about this poem's form?
   (1) The number of words changes from line to line.
   (2) The lines gradually get longer from first to last, like stairs.
   (3) Each line is a sentence.
   (4) The poet left extra space after some words to make a point.

4. What is the rhyme pattern of the first verse?
   (1) It doesn't rhyme.
   (2) Lines 1 and 3 rhyme, and lines 2 and 4 rhyme.
   (3) Lines 2 and 5 rhyme, and lines 3 and 4 rhyme.
   (4) The first and last lines rhyme.

5. What is the rhyme pattern of the second verse?
   (1) Lines 6 and 7 rhyme.
   (2) Lines 6 and 8 rhyme.
   (3) Lines 7 and 9 rhyme, and lines 10 and 11 rhyme.
   (4) Lines 6, 8, and 10 rhyme.

6. What picture does the poem paint in your mind?
   (1) birds standing around shivering, waiting to eat
   (2) a tray on top of the snow that has all different shapes and colors of seeds
   (3) a big gray squirrel "elbowing his way" to the food tray
   (4) all of the above

7. What metaphor can you see in the overall meaning of the poem?
   (1) The squirrel is a bully.
   (2) The birds are many different kinds of people.
   (3) The birdfeeder is the planet Earth.
   (4) The person who feeds the birds is God.

8. In what season does the poem take place? How do you know?
   (1) The poem mentions summer and sand.
   (2) The poem mentions spring and birds.
   (3) The poem mentions winter and snow.
   (4) The poem mentions fall and leaves.

Check your answers on page 162.

UNIT 4

Reading Short Fiction

SHORT STORIES are a form of **fiction**. They are made-up stories. The writer uses imagination to describe people, places, and events that are not real.

Most stories have at least one character, a setting, a plot, a conflict, and a theme. The **characters** are the people in the story. The **setting** is where and when the story takes place. The **plot** is the series of events that makes up the story. The **conflict** is the problem that the characters face. The **theme** is the message about life that the writer wants readers to understand. Using hints and clues in the story to figure out what the writer wants you to understand is part of the fun of reading fiction.

The main purpose of reading fiction is pleasure. A good story entertains you. It also gives you a look at how other people live. Reading fiction lets you share their experiences and feelings.

Chapter	What You Will Learn About	What You Will Read
12	Characters	"The Eyes of Mr. Lovides"
13	Setting	"An American Twenty"
14	Plot	"Tom Sawyer, the Pirate"
15	Conflict	"The Man and the Snake"
16	Theme	"The Adventure of the Three Students"
Review	Reading Short Fiction	"The Cop and the Anthem"

After reading this unit, you should be able to

- understand how characters are developed in a story

- identify the plot of a story

- identify the conflict in a story

- determine the theme of a story

Chapter 12

Characters

When you really get involved in a work of fiction, the story unfolds in your mind like a movie on a screen. You use your imagination and the writer's clues to create pictures in your mind.

The **characters** are the people in the story. These people can be just like people you know. Or they can be people who are different from anyone you have met in real life. They can even be aliens from the far future. What all good characters have in common is that you care about them. This makes you care about what happens in the story.

Think about how you react when you meet someone for the first time. You notice details such as how the person is dressed and how the person talks. You use these clues to decide whether you like this person. Writers do the same thing in fiction. They give you enough information about a character so you can decide how you feel about the character. Writers do this in two ways. They describe a character's physical appearance and personality. They also tell you how the character acts and what the character says.

The following short story is about a fictional character named Herb Stone. Use the details of his appearance and the way he behaves to form a picture of Herb in your mind.

Hot Herb

Herb looked in the men's room mirror as he combed his hair. He could still cover his bald spot, but just barely. Maybe it was time to get a hairpiece. What woman would want a middle-aged, middle-income guy with a bald spot and a beer belly?

"Cut it out," he said to himself. "This is no time to lose your confidence." He put the comb into his pocket, sucked in his stomach, and walked out to the bar. "Come on, girls," he yelled above the music. "I'm hot tonight. And I'm buying the drinks."

Pam looked at Herb as he sat down next to her. She thought, "Here comes another loudmouth. Just what I need."

But Herb said, "Hi. I'm Herb Stone. You look like you've had a hard day. Can I buy you a drink?"

As they talked, Herb and Pam realized they had a lot in common. They not only lived in the same part of the city, but they also both worked downtown. Herb relaxed and dropped his "Mr. Confidence" act. Pam liked how comfortable she felt with Herb. She discovered they both enjoyed old movies, walks along the lake, Thai food, and garage sales. Pam decided Herb might be okay after all.

◆ **Answer these questions about the short story "Hot Herb."**

Which words tell you how Herb looks? _____

You are right if you wrote **middle-aged, bald spot,** and **beer belly.**

From what Herb says and does, how does he feel about his appearance?

_____

Herb tries to hide his bald spot and suck in his stomach. This shows that **Herb doesn't like how he looks.** His words "This is no time to lose your confidence" and "I'm buying the drinks" confirm that he's not sure women will like him for himself.

What does Pam think about Herb when she first meets him?

_____

You are correct if you said Pam thinks Herb is a **loudmouthed guy.**

At the end of the story, how do Pam's thoughts and feelings about Herb change?

_____

You are right if you wrote Pam realizes that **she and Herb have a lot in common.**

Strategy: Understanding Characters

- Picture the characters in your mind as you read descriptions of their physical appearance.
- Notice how the characters act, what they say, and how they say it. How does this information add to your picture?
- Notice what others in the story say and think about a character.

Exercise

It is said that "the eyes are the windows of the soul." Why are the eyes of Mr. Lovides important to this story?

Read the story and answer the questions.

LANGUAGE Tip

Mr. Lovides   loh VEE des

Knowing how to pronounce characters' names makes reading a story more enjoyable.

The Eyes of Mr. Lovides

by John Godey

It was a quarter to ten, and the breakfast was over. But Joey **dawdled,**[1] inventing aimless tasks for himself, dreading the moment when he would have to approach Mr. Lovides, although Frank had assured him there would be no difficulty.

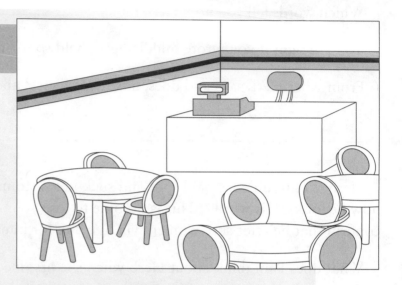

Even after a year in the employ of Mr. Lovides, Joey still feared him. Mr. Lovides had olive skin (much darker than Joey's own) and hollow cheeks with sharply etched lines. He was a **taciturn**[2] man who never smiled.

But it was the eyes of Mr. Lovides that made Joey afraid. They were black eyes, not bright and polished as eyes should be, but like **pitch,**[3] set deep and hot in the bony sockets. Joey did not understand these eyes; they appeared always to be threatening. He had mentioned this once to Frank. Frank had laughed and said that in his opinion the eyes of Mr. Lovides seemed rather gentle and compassionate.

Joey glanced at the clock once more and became panicky. If he did not leave soon he would be late, and the ceremony would be delayed.

He straightened his shoulders, wiped his moist hands on his apron and walked forward on the slat platform to the cashier's desk at the front of the luncheonette. Mr. Lovides sat behind the desk, with a sheaf of statements and his big checkbook before him. He looked up at Joey.

Joey's gaze wavered before Mr. Lovides's flat stare. He wet his lips with his tongue and managed to blurt out, "Frank said he speak to you, ask you to let me off for his marriage. To be witness."

---

[1] **dawdled:** moved slowly
[2] **taciturn:** quiet, not talkative
[3] **pitch:** black tar

LANGUAGE Tip

Puerto Rico is an island in the Caribbean Sea. It is located east of Mexico and north of Venezuela. Puerto Ricans are U.S. citizens. However, Puerto Ricans cannot vote for the U.S. president.

Mr. Lovides's lids flickered for a moment, concealing his eyes. "Be back by eleven-thirty," he said.

Joey turned away quickly and went back to the kitchen. He dressed swiftly but with care, putting on the powder-blue suit with the thin stripes running through the cloth like rich veins of gold.

Mr. Lovides did not look up from the cashier's desk as he hurried by.

Joey waited impatiently on the el[4] platform for a train. When it came, he took a seat beside a window.

The train moved rapidly in its halting, deceptively antiquated[5] way, and in another ten minutes it would be there. The realization that he would soon be seeing Frank for the last time filled his eyes with sudden tears. He brushed them away angrily. A wedding day was not a day for tears, but for rejoicing.

Yet for Joey it was a day of sorrow. Without Frank he could not hope to hold the job of counterman. Soon he would be back in the sweaty kitchen again.

In the beginning he had not minded the dishwashing. He had left Puerto Rico only a week before he got the job. Any job was fine which would pay enough to live on, to buy the splendid, sharp clothing worn by his compatriots[6] in the States. The trays heaped with soiled dishes were a heavy load. The smells of the kitchen were sometimes overpowering. The hot, greasy dishwater reddened and wrinkled his hands. But it had seemed a fine job—then.

He could not now recall the first time Frank had spoken to him. Joey's English had been very poor then, and he would not have understood Frank anyway. But he did understand the friendly tone of Frank's voice and the warm smile of this tall counterman with the blond, unruly hair. It was the first friendliness he had encountered in the teeming,[7] hostile city.

He cherished the countless instances of Frank's warmth and helpfulness, but the most memorable of all came on the day Ralph, the second counterman, quit. Frank went to Mr. Lovides and asked him to try Joey at the job. Mr. Lovides had ● first been unwilling to do this, but he had much respect for Frank. The next morning Joey came out of the kitchen and took his place proudly behind the second counter.

Joey was polite and cheerful, and he soon built up his own circle of special customers. Many of them were girls—stenographers and clerks from the big office buildings—who enjoyed making him blush by remarking on his long black eyelashes.

[4]el: a city railroad that runs on an "elevated" track
[5]antiquated: old
[6]compatriots: fellow countrymen
[7]teeming: crowded

Oh, it was a wonderful job. He was no longer a menial, unskilled boy from Puerto Rico, but a personage of some importance. . . .

The train had come into the City Hall Station. Joey got out and went slowly down the stairs to the street. Even now, he found it hard to believe that Frank was going away, though he had known for a long time that his friend planned to be married and then return to his home in Worcester to live.

As Frank's last day at the luncheonette came closer, Joey had grown increasingly **morose.**[8] He had even been rude to one of his regular customers. Mr. Lovides had witnessed the incident. He said nothing, but the look in his eyes had burned fear into Joey's heart. The fear was still with him as he entered the building where Frank was waiting. . . .

The marriage didn't take long. A white-haired man intoned the phrases, while Frank and his girl looked at each other with glistening eyes. Frank and his new wife smiled at Joey warmly and insisted that he come up to Worcester often to visit them. He stood there and nodded, his eyes filled with tears, the smile on his lips fixed and stiff. Then they were gone, and he walked back to the el and returned to the luncheonette.

His legs trembled as he opened the door and went in. His eyes picked out the wall clock: 11:25. He started toward the kitchen and then stopped, as abruptly as though he had come up against an invisible barrier. Behind the counter—the second counter, *his* counter—there was another man, wearing a fresh linen jacket.

For a long time Joey stood still, feeling the heat of unreleased tears behind his blinking lids. Nor did he move when Mr. Lovides came out of the kitchen and walked toward him.

He was only dimly aware of Mr. Lovides's voice: "Got a new man to work the second counter . . ."

It had happened already, so soon. The very day of Frank's departure he had become again a Puerto Rican boy of no **consequence,**[9] fit only for the kitchen, the greasy suds. Without Frank, he was nothing.

The eyes of Mr. Lovides drilled into him, but his voice was lost in the roaring that filled Joey's ears. A wave of self-pitying resentment surged up in him. But suddenly Mr. Lovides's voice penetrated Joey's **anguish.**[10] Joey stared at him in disbelief.

Mr. Lovides, somewhat impatiently, repeated himself: "So from now on you work the first counter. Understand?"

---

[8]**morose:** sad
[9]**consequence:** importance
[10]**anguish:** pain

Joey could not trust himself to reply. He nodded his head in **mute**,[11] overwhelming happiness. Now he could bear the going away of Frank, now he could bear anything that might come. He was no longer an **alien**,[12] but a man who could stand alone, in confidence and pride. He had lost much today, when Frank had gone away. But he had gained even more than he had lost.

Before starting for the kitchen, Joey looked directly into the eyes of Mr. Lovides. They were gentle, compassionate eyes, and he was astonished that he could ever have feared them.

---

[11]**mute:** silent

[12]**alien:** foreigner

1. How many characters are named and well described in the story?
   (1) one
   (2) two
   (3) three
   (4) four

2. What does Joey think of Mr. Lovides at the beginning of the story?
   (1) Mr. Lovides is frightening.
   (2) Mr. Lovides is kind.
   (3) Mr. Lovides is sad.
   (4) Mr. Lovides is stupid.

3. In the last three paragraphs of the story, what does Joey realize about Mr. Lovides?
   (1) Mr. Lovides is cruel.
   (2) Mr. Lovides is shy.
   (3) Mr. Lovides is kind.
   (4) Mr. Lovides is prejudiced.

4. Frank does not share Joey's original opinion of Mr. Lovides. How does Frank describe Mr. Lovides's eyes?
   (1) mean and threatening
   (2) black as pitch
   (3) concealed
   (4) gentle and compassionate

5. What kind of person is Frank?
   (1) warm and friendly
   (2) a bully
   (3) shy and quiet
   (4) prejudiced against Puerto Ricans

6. Which trait does *not* describe Joey?
   (1) insecure
   (2) Puerto Rican
   (3) shy
   (4) confident

7. What kind of clothes does Joey like?
   (1) jeans and T-shirts
   (2) leather jackets
   (3) sharp, dressy clothes
   (4) He's not interested in clothes.

8. The next-to-last paragraph says Joey "had gained even more than he had lost." What does Joey gain at the end of the story?
   (1) money
   (2) confidence and pride
   (3) a wife
   (4) knowledge of how to fight

9. Which trait does *not* describe Frank?
   (1) long black eyelashes
   (2) tall
   (3) blond hair
   (4) unruly hair

10. What four actions from the story show Mr. Lovides's compassion?

_____

_____

11. What clue in paragraph 6 tells you that Joey is new to this country?

_____

Check your answers on pages 163–164.

Writing Workshop

Prewriting
Make a list of people you know. Choose one person to write about.

Note as many facts as you can about that person. List details about his or her physical appearance, emotions, personality, family, friends, job, and interests. Try to use similes and metaphors in your descriptive notes. For example, "Lisa's eyes shine like the sun."

Drafting
Write a paragraph or two describing your character. Tell what your character looks like. Include details about what your character says, does, and thinks.

Revising
Be sure your description has a logical order. Perhaps the first paragraph will describe what the person looks like, and the second paragraph will describe how the person acts.

Editing
The tense of a verb tells time. If you are describing a living person, you may use present-tense verbs throughout your essay. However, if you are describing someone who is no longer living, you may use past-tense verbs. Look at the tense of each verb in your essay and make sure it shows the correct time.

Chapter 13

Setting

Just as you picture characters in your mind, you also picture a story's setting as you read. The **setting** of a story is the time and place in which its events occur. For example, the story might take place at the beach during the summer or in a hospital late at night.

A story may be set in a real place or in a place the writer has made up. It may be set in the past, the present, or the future. Sometimes the setting is named at the beginning of the story. But at other times, you must infer (or figure out) the setting from the story's details.

Read the following paragraph. Look for information about the setting of this story.

Ohio Plowgirl

Lydia mopped her sweaty face with her handkerchief. She could see the heat rise in waves from the cornfield. It was surprisingly hot for a spring day. And she had been plowing the field for hours. The horses that pulled the plow were tired too. Lydia remembered the days when her biggest job was to cook for her father and brothers when they came in from planting. But two years ago the Civil War had started, and now it seemed all the men in Ohio were in the army. Lydia and her mother and her little sisters needed corn to eat and to feed the cows. To keep from starving, they had to do the work themselves.

◆ **Answer these questions about the setting of this story.**

1. Where does the story take place?

   _____

2. During what season of the year does the story take place?

   _____

3. Write the sentence that helped you answer question #2.

   _____

4. During what time of day does the story take place?

   _____

5. Write the sentence that helped you answer question #4.

   _____

6. The Civil War took place from 1861 to 1865. In what year does the story take place?

   _____

7. Write the clue from the story that helped you answer question #6.

   _____

Here are the answers to the questions:

1. on a farm in Ohio
2. spring
3. It was surprisingly hot for a spring day.
4. late morning or afternoon
5. And she had been plowing the field for hours.
6. 1863
7. Two years ago the Civil War had started.

Strategy: Understanding Setting

- Look for words that tell you where the story is set. Indoors or out? City or country? A real place or a made-up place?

- Look for words that tell you when the story takes place. What year? What season? What time of day?

Exercise

The term *ugly American* describes Americans in a foreign country whose behavior offends the people of that country. What do the people in this story think of the American tourists?

LANGUAGE Tip

Here is how to pronounce the Spanish names in this story.

Miguel	mee GEL
Juana	WAH nah
Carreras	car RAY ras

Read the story and answer the questions.

An American Twenty

by Pamela Hathaway Harrer

"I told you already I was listening, Miguel." Juana Carreras glanced down at her middle child. Shadows of laundry and leaves shifted over the bare dirt as a thick breeze moved behind the bark-walled house. Juana ran one hand through her sweat-dampened hair. Several chickens scratched just inside the doorway. Juana rested her hands on her hips as she stared at them. Only one egg today. She turned back to the wire and draped a girl's yellow dress, lightly bunched, between the barbs. Cool water dropped on Juana's feet.

"Mama, listen!" Miguel kicked up a small cloud of dust with his toes.

"Miguel, what?" She needed more water. Both ten-gallon cans were almost dry. Juana turned to her nine-year-old. "Your pants are filthy. Here, give them to me so Marta can wash them." Juana pulled a damp pair of shorts out of the tree beside her for her son to put on. A moment later, she threw his salt-stiff pants into a tin basin filled with soapy gray water several feet away. "Why are you back?"

"I'm telling you! I went to the . . ."

"You can get more water as long as you're here, then." Juana raised her voice as she turned toward the doorway. "Marta, I want you to wash the little ones now. Miguel is here to help you carry water."

The eldest, Marta, stepped out of the darkness nudging her four-year-old brother ahead of her with her knee. She held a **listless**[1] baby under her arm and pulled

---

[1]**listless:** lacking the energy to move

LANGUAGE Tip

The Dominican Republic is located southeast of Cuba. It is the eastern two-thirds of the island of Hispaniola. The country has more than 800 miles of beautiful beaches.

another slightly older one behind her. She struggled briefly to **disentangle**[2] the baby from her long ponytail before settling the children in the shade under the palm.

Miguel tugged on the pocket of his mother's worn blue dress. "Mama, I went to the beach by the pink hotel today, the one that Papa helped to build, where the sand is soft . . ."

Juana batted his hand. "You didn't swim there . . ."

"I didn't. But I . . ."

"You swim on our side if you need water." Juana's voice was hard.

Miguel looked at the ground. "The rocks cut."

Juana crossed her arms over her broad chest. She remembered, before the hotels, sinking into the smooth wet sand, sifting it between her toes. Roberto's work on the pink one had fed them. She fed the children herself now, since Roberto had been killed in a construction accident on a site at the edge of town.

Miguel shifted his weight from foot to foot in the soft dust of the yard as Juana regarded him. She sighed. "There's no time for swimming on either side of the bay today, Miguel."

"But listen! I was the first boy down today, and I got the first tourists I saw to hire me."

Juana nodded. She had Miguel make only three trips to the well by the blue church for water in the morning, so he could get to the beach early. There weren't always enough tourists in the late summer for so many boys. Her two girls between him and Marta carried the rest of the water, before following him to the beach with baskets of mangoes and oranges to sell for three **Dominican pesos**[3] each.

Palms rustled as the heavy breeze changed directions. The sour smell of sewage drifted over them from the narrow flow at the end of the road.

Miguel pulled again on his mother's skirt. "There were two of them, Mama, a man and a woman. Americanos, they said."

A drop of sweat rolled down Juana's neck. She was almost out of rice.

"The man went away in a boat with the fisherman, and . . ."

Juana looked at the sky. She'd woven another sheet of bark under the hole in the roof from the inside. Would it still leak?

" . . . the lady stayed. She couldn't understand me, except a few words, but we made pictures in the sand to talk."

---

[2]**disentangle:** to free from
[3]**Dominican pesos:** money used in the Dominican Republic

The goat, Lupita, strained against the rope that held her near the house. Juana reminded herself to have one of the children milk her later.

"It was too hot for the lady, so she went in the water all the time, and I stayed on the end of her chair with her bag while she was gone . . ."

"You're a good boy, Miguel. Now Marta needs your help."

"Mama! She was gone for a long time once when she did the parachute behind the boat and . . ."

Juana slapped at a fly on her arm, then rested the back of her hand over her eyes. Waves crashed rhythmically against the rocks below the dump two roads away.

"Each time she came back I washed the sand off her feet with sea water from my bottle, and I put oil on her back . . ."

Marta made a path in the ground as she dragged a brown plastic basin through the dirt toward her mother. She stopped beside the laundry pile. One by one, she **retrieved**[4] her **charges**[5] from the spot where she'd propped them, and fit them into the small, high-sided tub. She emptied the last inch of water from the nearest can into the tub over the children, then replaced it in the dirt. She did the same with the second.

Juana's stomach burned. "Did you eat today, Miguel?"

"She got pizza and Coca-Cola from the hotel for me, and when she got sand in hers, she gave me that, too."

"Good." Juana reached down for a frayed, wet towel.

Marta scanned the yard. "There's no more water, Mama."

"Use that," Juana pointed with her bare foot toward the low tin basin nearby, "and Miguel is going to get you more. Don't use any more soap."

Marta lifted the basin with both hands. She staggered several steps, rested it on the edge of the tub, then flooded the children with laundry water. Miguel's shorts sunk between them.

"Mama," Miguel said, "she asked me if I went to school."

"School!" Juana shook her head. A gull screamed in the distance.

"The man came back, and he swam, too, and I washed his feet, too. Not the lady. I stayed on the end of her chair. She just closed her eyes, but she didn't go to sleep."

"Miguel, after you've gotten water, I need you to catch some of the chickens."

"As soon as the man went to sleep, she got up and went through her bag. She kept looking at the man, but he stayed asleep."

Juana noticed for the first time the fists he held tightly clenched against his chest.

---

[4]**retrieved:** found and brought back
[5]**charges:** those one takes care of

"She put her finger over her lips at me, and then . . ." Miguel slowly opened one hand, "she gave me this."

Juana took the balled-up paper. Her eyes widened as she gently flattened out the green bill. **Veinte**.[6] An American twenty. She held her breath as she stared at it, then in one motion exhaled and stuffed it into the pocket without the hole. Rice. Kerosene.

"The man woke up and when they left, he gave me this." Miguel handed his mother a ten-peso coin, from his other fist, that she slipped into the same pocket.

"You did well, Miguel. You keep them happy. Now go get water for your sister so I can finish hanging the wash." Juana's heart pounded as she turned back to the pile by her feet. A plane passed by overhead.

Miguel scooped two plastic water buckets from a pile next to the door. He leapt across the foul stream at the end of the road, then disappeared toward the well.

Juana carefully arranged a small shirt on the wire, imagining for a moment it was one of the stiff white shirts the children wear to school. She imagined hanging alongside it the dark navy pants school boys wear. Juana remembered the blue jumper she'd worn as a girl for two years, when her family could pay, before she was needed back at home. Juana always needed all of her children who were old enough to walk.

A baby cried out—Juana knew without looking it wasn't hers. She reached into her pocket to feel the paper again. Two hundred forty pesos on the black market. Medicine.

Miguel appeared shortly and gave the bottles to Marta, then stood back quietly watching as she sat each child on the edge of the tub. Marta poured the rinse water over them separately. Juana turned when the smallest whimpered and coughed. The older two giggled as they slipped back into the dirty water of the tub.

"Come here, Miguel," Juana called.

Miguel shuffled through crushed leaves and bits of bark to his mother.

Juana took him firmly by the shoulders. "What did you say to the lady when she asked you about school?"

"I told her, Mama, it costs too much money." Miguel grinned.

Juana held him tightly so he couldn't get away as she kissed his forehead. "You're a smart boy."

---

[6]**veinte** (VAYN tay): Spanish for "twenty"

1. At what time of the year does this story take place? _____

2. Where is "An American Twenty" set? List clues that tell you the setting.

   _____

   ● _____

3. List five clues that tell you this story is set in a warm climate.

   _____

   _____

4. List five clues that tell you the Carreras family lives in poverty.

   _____

   _____

5. Does Miguel speak English? How do you know?

   _____

6. What clues tell you that one of the children is sick?

   _____

7. Did the woman want the man to know that she had given Miguel $20? How do you know?

   _____

8. Why doesn't Miguel go to school? _____

9. The world of the Carreras family is contrasted with the world of the two tourists. Use the chart below to show the contrasts between these worlds. The first example is done for you.

	Carreras Family	Tourists
beach	rocky, dangerous	smooth, soft, sandy, safe
housing		
ways each spends time		
food		

Check your answers on page 164.

Writing Workshop

Prewriting
Think of events in your own life that remind you of this story. Have you ever had luck like Miguel's $20 bill? Choose one episode to write about.

Picture in your mind the event you have chosen. Where did it take place? When did it take place? What year was it? What season? What time of day?

Drafting
Write a paragraph about the event. Use the details you've listed to describe the setting.

Revising
Ask a friend to read your paragraph. Was the setting described well enough to create a picture in his or her mind? Is the year, season, and time of day clear?

Editing
Look for short sentences that can be combined so they are more interesting. Example:
- The street was dark. The moon wasn't very bright.
- The street was dark because the moon was behind a cloud.

Chapter 14

Plot

If you tell a friend about a movie you saw last night, you will probably spend most of your time describing the plot of the movie. The **plot** is the series of events in a story. Telling about the plot answers the question "What happened in the story?"

If Ricardo meets Emily, that is an event. But suppose Ricardo meets Emily, falls in love with her, has a fight with her, and then wins her back. That is a plot. As you can tell from this example, the plot depends on characters. The plot cannot exist without people. What actions take place depends on what the characters are like.

Plot also depends on conflict. At the beginning of the story, the main characters are introduced. Then the plot focuses on a character's problem and the action he or she takes to solve that problem. The action of a good story builds to a turning point, or climax. The climax is the part of the story where the character's problem is solved. Then the story ends, or comes to a conclusion.

Every plot has these four basic parts: a beginning, a problem (or conflict), a climax, and a conclusion. These parts lead you through the story and keep you interested in what will happen next.

| Beginning | $\longrightarrow$ | Problem | $\longrightarrow$ | Climax | $\longrightarrow$ | Conclusion |

"High School Flame" is a brief story. A real story would be longer, and it would have many details. The plot would also be woven together with more details about the characters and setting.

High School Flame

Eric and Beth dated all through high school. Then they had a fight about something silly and broke up. A few years later, Eric heard Beth had gotten married. Eric's friends kept fixing him up with attractive women, but nothing ever worked out. Eric compared all the women to Beth.

One day Eric was shopping at the supermarket when he saw Beth. She looked as beautiful as ever. When Eric spoke to Beth, she was friendly, but she seemed in a hurry. She said she had to take one of her kids to soccer practice and feed the other two.

Maybe she's divorced, Eric thought. He asked about her husband. "He is great. He is out of town for a few days, and I miss him so much! You'd think we were still teenagers. Remember how intense everything felt at that age?" Yeah, I remember, thought Eric.

Eric said good-bye to Beth and took his one lonely pork chop to the checkout counter.

◆ **Answer these questions about "High School Flame."**

The story begins with a brief history of Eric and Beth's relationship as teenagers. The problem is that Eric, after many years, is still in love with Both.

What do you think is the climax of this story?

_____

You are right if you said **Beth tells Eric she is happily married.**

What is the conclusion, or end, of the story?

_____

You are correct if you wrote **Eric said good-bye to Beth and took his pork chop to the checkout counter.**

Strategy: Identifying Plot

- At the beginning, make mental pictures of the characters.
- Notice the problem that the characters must solve.
- Identify the climax by asking "What is the most exciting point in the story?" or "Where is the problem solved?"
- Look for the conclusion, which brings the story to an end.

Exercise

This famous story is from Mark Twain's novel *Tom Sawyer*. Would you have done what Tom did when he thought he was not loved?

Read the story and complete the exercises.

Tom Sawyer, the Pirate

Adapted from the novel
by Mark Twain

Tom's mind was made up now. Nobody loved him. When they found out what they had driven him to, perhaps they would be sorry. They had forced him to lead a life of crime. There was no choice.

By this time, he was far down Meadow Lane. He sobbed when he heard the bell for school. He would never, never hear that old familiar sound any more.

Just at that point, he met Joe Harper. Joe had been coming to find Tom. His mother had whipped him for drinking some cream which he had never tasted. It was plain that she was tired of him and wished him to go away. He hoped she would be happy that she had driven her poor boy out into the world to suffer and die.

The two boys walked along. They made a promise to stand by each other. Then they began to lay their plans. They decided to become pirates.

Three miles down the Mississippi River was a long wooded island. No one lived there. So they chose Jackson Island as the place where they would be pirates. Then they hunted up Huckleberry Finn, who joined them at once. They would meet at midnight and go to the island.

When Tom woke up the next morning, he wondered where he was. He looked around. There was a delicious sense of peace and silence in the woods. Tom stirred

LANGUAGE Tip

Mark Twain is the pen name for Samuel Clemens (1835–1910). Clemens grew up near the Mississippi River. As a young man, he worked on a riverboat. Many of his stories take place along the Mississippi River.

the other pirates. In a minute they were chasing each other and tumbling over each other in the shallow water. They felt no longing for the little village sleeping in the distance. They found plenty of things to be delighted with. And they took a swim every hour. But by the middle of the afternoon, a sense of loneliness began to fall on the boys, though none was brave enough to speak his thought.

By afternoon the boys became conscious of a peculiar sound in the distance. "What is it!" exclaimed Joe, under his breath.

"I wonder," said Tom in a whisper. "Listen—don't talk."

The boys sprang to their feet and hurried to the shore. They hid behind the bushes and looked out. A little steam ferryboat was about a mile below the village.

"I know now!" exclaimed Tom. "Somebody's drownded!"

"That's it!" said Huck. "They done that last summer. They shot a cannon over the water and that makes a body come up to the top."

The boys listened and watched. Then an idea flashed through Tom's mind, and he exclaimed, "Boys, I know who's drownded—it's us!"

They felt like heroes in an instant. They were missed. They were **mourned**.[1] Hearts were breaking on their account. Tears were being shed. This was fine. It was worthwhile to be a pirate, after all.

That night, after Joe and Huck had fallen asleep, Tom snuck back to the village. Shortly he found himself at his aunt's back fence. In the house sat Polly, Sid, Mary, and Joe Harper's mother. Tom went to the door and pressed it open gently. Quickly he hid under Aunt Polly's bed.

"He wasn't so BAD—only mischEEvous. HE never meant any harm," said Aunt Polly, and then she began to cry.

"It was just so with my Joe—always up to every kind of mischief. But he was just as kind as he could be. And to think I whipped him for taking that cream, when I throwed it out myself because it was sour. And I will never see him again in this world, never, never, poor boy." And Mrs. Harper sobbed as if her heart would break.

Tom went on listening. It was guessed that the boys had drowned while taking a swim. This was Wednesday night. If the bodies continued missing until Sunday, all hope would be given up. The funerals would be preached on that morning.

---

[1]**mourned:** wept for

[After Mrs. Harper left and Aunt Polly went to sleep, Tom made his way back to the island. The boys spent the next three days hunting for turtles, lying in the hot sand, and playing marbles. They swam and chased each other. Now and then they looked longingly at the village across the river. When Joe and Huck decided they wanted to stop being pirates, Tom told them he knew their funeral was being planned. Meanwhile, the boys' families and other members of the town continued to mourn the boys.]

On Sunday, when the Sunday-school hour was finished, a bell began to **toll**,[2] instead of ringing in the usual way. It was a very quiet Sabbath, and the sound of the bell seemed in keeping with the hush. The villagers began to gather, loitering a moment to talk in whispers about the sad event. But there was no whispering in the church. The only sound was the rustling of dresses as the women went to their seats. None could remember when the little church had been so full before.

There was finally a waiting pause. Then Aunt Polly entered, followed by Sid and Mary. Then came the Harper family, all in deep black. The whole congregation, the old minister as well, rose and stood until the mourners were seated in the front pew. There was another silence, broken only by muffled sobs. Then the minister spread his hands and prayed. A moving hymn was sung and a Bible text was read.

As the service proceeded, the minister spoke of the graces, the winning ways, and the rare promise of the lost lads. Everyone in the church felt a little guilty about having seen only the boys' faults. The minister told many a touching story that illustrated their sweet nature. The people could easily see, now, how noble and beautiful those boys were. And they remembered with grief that at the time they had seemed like rascals.

The congregation became more and more moved. At last everyone broke down and cried with the mourners. The preacher himself began to cry in the pulpit.

There was a noise in the balcony, which nobody noticed. A moment later, the church door creaked. The minister raised his eyes above his handkerchief and stood amazed! First one and then another pair of eyes followed the minister's eyes. Then the congregation rose and stared while the three dead boys came marching up the aisle. Tom was in the lead, Joe next, and finally Huck. They had hid in the unused balcony, listening to their own funeral sermon!

Aunt Polly, Mary, and the Harpers threw themselves upon Tom and Joe. They smothered the boys with kisses and poured out thanksgiving. Poor Huck stood uncomfortable, not knowing exactly what to do or where to hide. He started to slink away, but Tom seized him and said, "Aunt Polly, it ain't fair. Somebody's got to be glad to see Huck."

---

[2]**toll:** ring slowly, usually to announce a death

"And so they shall. I'm glad to see him, poor motherless thing!" And the attention Aunt Polly gave him made him more uncomfortable than he was before.

Suddenly the minister shouted at the top of his voice: "Praise God from whom all blessings flow—SING!—and put your hearts in it!"

And they did. Tom Sawyer the Pirate looked around and confessed in his heart that this was the proudest moment of his life.

PART A

Number the events of the story in the correct time order.

_____ A ferryboat fires off cannons to look for the drowned boys.

_____ Tom decides to leave home and become a pirate.

_____ Tom has never felt better in his life.

_____ Tom hears Aunt Polly say that a funeral is planned for Sunday.

_____ The minister describes the boys as sweet and beautiful.

_____ The boys spend three days swimming and playing on the island.

PART B

Circle the best answer for each question.

1. Who is the main character in the story?
   (1) Tom Sawyer
   (2) Joe Harper
   (3) Huckleberry Finn
   (4) Aunt Polly

2. What problem is Tom trying to solve?
   (1) He must find a way to help his friend Joe run away from home.
   (2) He cannot find his friend Huckleberry Finn.
   (3) He does not feel loved.
   (4) He will never hear the school bell again.

3. Which place is NOT the setting of part of this story?
   (1) Aunt Polly's bedroom
   (2) the church
   (3) the school
   (4) the island

4. Why are Aunt Polly and Mrs. Harper spending the evening together?
   (1) Their boys are both missing.
   (2) They are neighbors who enjoy spending time together.
   (3) Mrs. Harper needs Aunt Polly's help to find Joe.
   (4) Aunt Polly knows where the lost cream is.

5. Which clue helps you understand the date of the story?
   (1) the school bell
   (2) the steam ferryboat
   (3) the peaceful woods on the island
   (4) the minister's sermon

6. What is the climax of the story?
   (1) Tom's finding out there would be a funeral on Sunday
   (2) Tom's listening to the sermon
   (3) Tom's being hugged by Aunt Polly
   (4) Tom's feeling proud of himself

7. Which of the following is NOT a clue that the boys will return home?
   (1) Tom realizes the villagers think they have drowned.
   (2) Tom sneaks back home to find out what is going on.
   (3) The boys get lonesome, but they won't admit it.
   (4) The boys look longingly at the village.

8. What do you learn from the story about Huck?
   (1) His mother is mad at him for taking the cream.
   (2) He often skips school.
   (3) He is much older than the other boys.
   (4) He has no family.

9. Which word is NOT used to describe the boys?
   (1) mischievous
   (2) smart
   (3) kind
   (4) rascal

10. Is the ending of "Tom Sawyer, the Pirate" effective? Why or why not?

_____

_____

Check your answers on page 165.

Writing Workshop

Prewriting

Think about a time when you jumped to the wrong conclusion. Maybe you assumed the worst about someone because he or she was different from you. Or maybe you gave somebody too much credit because he or she was attractive or wealthy. Then choose one incident to write about.

Make notes about how you felt when you realized that you had misjudged this person. Did you feel ashamed of making a judgment when you didn't really know the person? Did you feel disappointed in yourself when you realized you had made a mistake? Later, did you just try to put the event out of your mind and pretend that it had never happened? Or did you go back to the person to try to explain why you reacted as you did?

Drafting

Write a paragraph describing the event and the way it made you feel. Tell what you did when you realized you were wrong.

Revising

In your essay, you want to describe an incident and tell how you felt later about the incident. Be sure the description of the incident contains all the details that your reader needs to understand how you felt later.

Editing

Use quotation marks around the exact words that someone says. Place periods and commas inside the quotation marks. Example:

- I said, "Marcus is loud and impolite."

Chapter 15

Conflict

When you hear the word *conflict*, you probably think of a fight. In a story, the **conflict** is the problem that the characters are trying to solve. The plot of a story is the series of actions that the characters take to solve the problem.

Conflict can be internal or external. An **internal conflict** is a struggle that takes place in a character's mind. The person must figure out what is the right thing to do and then decide whether to do it. An example is a child in a store who wants a toy. He has no money, and he knows that stealing is wrong. Does he satisfy his urge, or does he do the right thing? That is an internal conflict.

An **external conflict** is a struggle between one or more characters and an outside force. That force might be another person, a sports team, or a whole town. In the movie *Star Wars,* the external conflict is between good guys and an entire universe. An external conflict can also be a struggle against a force of nature, such as an earthquake or a fire.

Whether internal or external, conflict is what makes the action of a story exciting. The conflict is usually introduced early in a story. The excitement that develops as you try to figure out how the problem will be solved is called **suspense**. As the tension builds, your interest builds too. You read on because you want to find out who won and how the problem was solved. The story's climax is that point where one of the forces wins.

As you read the following story, decide what conflict the main character faces. Notice the steps she takes to solve the problem. Would you handle the conflict the same way?

Harassed

One night Gloria's boss, Henry, asked her to work late. "I'm sorry, but I can't. I'm busy tonight," she said.

"But we have to finish these financial statements by tomorrow, and you're my best worker. Could you stay just until 6 o'clock?" Henry asked.

Gloria agreed. At 5:00 p.m. her coworkers went home. Gloria stayed at her desk and continued checking figures. Then Henry came out of his office. "What a day," he said, rubbing his neck. "I need a massage."

"About this income statement," Gloria said quickly. "Isn't the decimal point in the wrong place?" She swiveled her computer screen to face Henry, but he moved it back and walked around behind her. He leaned over her shoulder. "You're right.

That should be millions of dollars, not thousands. I told you I needed you." Henry began to rub Gloria's shoulders. "Feels like you need a massage too. Relax."

Gloria froze. She wanted to roll her chair over his foot, but instead she said, "I really have to go now." She grabbed her purse and ran out of the door.

◆ **Answer these questions about "Harassed."**

Whom does Gloria have a conflict with?

_____

You are right if you said **her boss, Henry.**

What is the conflict about?

_____

You might have written **sexual harassment** or **the boss's attitude toward Gloria.**

Is the conflict internal or external?

_____

This is an **external conflict.** It is between Gloria and another person. But there is also an **internal conflict.** Gloria must decide how to handle Henry's advances.

Strategy: Identifying Conflict

- Look for the problem that the characters face.
- Decide whether the conflict is internal or external.
- Identify the steps that characters take to solve their problem.
- See whether these steps lead to other problems.

Exercise

LANGUAGE Tip

This story takes place in San Francisco, California. It became an important city when gold was discovered in California in 1848. Today the city is well known as the home of the Golden Gate Bridge.

Can reading a book make you think about ideas you do not usually think about?

Read the story and answer the questions.

The Man and the Snake

Adapted from the story by Ambrose Bierce

"It has been reported by the wise and learned that the eye of a serpent is like a magnet. Anyone who falls into its vision will be pulled toward its eye and will die from the serpent's bite."

Harker Brayton lay stretched at ease upon a sofa. He smiled as he read from old Morryster's *Marvels of Science.* He wondered how anyone could believe such nonsense.

Brayton was a man of thought. As he began thinking about the many ideas in this book, he lowered his book and his eyes wandered about the room. Suddenly he saw something in a corner of the room. In the shadow under his bed, there were two small points of light. The points were about an inch apart. Brayton gave little thought to what he'd seen. He continued reading.

A moment later something made him lower the book again. He looked toward the corner of the room. The points of light were still there. They seemed to be brighter than before. He saw a greenish light he hadn't noticed before. Then he thought that the lights might have moved a little nearer.

Brayton went back to reading. Suddenly something in the book suggested a thought that made him jump. He dropped his book for the third time. Brayton sat up a little. He stared beneath the bed. The points of light seemed to be shining with added fire. The lights were all he could think about. Directly beneath the foot of the bed was a large serpent. The points of light were its eyes! The serpent's head was directed straight toward him. Its wide jaw looked evil. Its eyes stared into his own eyes.

LANGUAGE Tip

Synonyms

These words mean the same as
distinguished:
   famous   well-known
   notable   respected

Harker Brayton was a 35-year-old bachelor. He was a scholar and something of an athlete. He was rich, popular, and healthy. He had recently returned to San Francisco after traveling to many countries. His friend, Dr. Druring, a distinguished scientist, had offered him a room. Dr. Druring's house was large and old-fashioned. One wing of the house was a combination laboratory, **menagerie,**[1] and museum. It was here that the doctor kept all forms of animal life. He particularly loved **reptiles.**[2] In spite of the animals, Brayton found the house very much to his liking.

Brayton was not familiar with reptiles. Was this snake dangerous? Was it poisonous?

Brayton rose to his feet and prepared to back softly away from the snake. He didn't want to disturb it, if possible. He knew that he could walk backward and find the door. In the meantime, the snake's eyes burned with more evil than ever.

"Nonsense!" he said aloud. "I am not a coward." He moved one foot, inch by inch, in front of the other. The snake had not moved. But its eyes were now electric sparks.

The man took a step forward, and another. And then he fell to the floor with a crash. He groaned. The snake made neither sound nor motion, but its eyes were two dazzling suns.

The man lay on the floor, within a yard of his enemy. He raised the upper part of his body upon his elbows. His face was white. There was froth upon his lips. Every movement he made left him a little nearer to the snake.

Dr. Druring and his wife sat in the library. Suddenly their conversation was interrupted by a mighty cry. They sprang to their feet. Almost before the echoes of the last cry had died away, the doctor was out of the room. He ran up the stairs, two at a time. In front of Brayton's chamber, he met some servants who had come from the upper floor. Together they rushed in the room without knocking.

Brayton lay upon his stomach on the floor, dead. His head and arms were partly under the bed. They pulled the body away, turning him upon his back. His eyes were wide open, staring—a dreadful sight.

"Died in a fit," said the scientist, bending his knee and placing his hand upon Brayton's heart. While in that position, he happened to glance under the bed. "Good God!" he added, "how did this thing get in here?"

He reached under the bed, pulled out the snake, and flung it to the center of the room. It slid across the polished floor till it stopped by the wall. There it lay without motion. It was a stuffed snake. Its eyes were two shoe buttons.

---

[1]**menagerie:** a collection of wild or foreign animals
[2]**reptiles:** animals such as snakes and lizards that move on their belly or on short legs

Chapter 15

PART A

1. What does Brayton read in an old book that he thinks is nonsense?

_____

2. Why is Dr. Druring's interest in animals important to the story?

_____

3. Why is the conclusion of the story unexpected?

_____

PART B

1. What is the main conflict in this story?
   (1) Brayton wants to trap the snake.
   (2) Brayton is living in a strange house.
   (3) Brayton is afraid of a snake.
   (4) Brayton is so tired that he keeps dropping his book.

2. What internal conflict does Brayton face?
   (1) Brayton does not want to look like he is afraid of the snake.
   (2) Brayton falls on the floor.
   (3) Brayton lives in a room all by himself.
   (4) Brayton cannot identify the type of snake he sees.

3. Why does Dr. Druring run so quickly when he hears the loud cry?
   (1) He thinks his house guest might have fallen down the stairs.
   (2) He knows he has dangerous snakes in the house.
   (3) He thinks a crime has been committed in the house.
   (4) He is worried that the servants will be disturbed.

4. What word best describes Brayton's state of mind?

   (1)   angry
   (2)   curious
   (3)   frightened
   (4)   confused

Check your answers on page 165.

Writing Workshop

Prewriting

Make a list of conflicts you face. Then decide whether each conflict is internal or external. For example, maybe you are juggling your job, child care, and housework. If so, you have the external conflict of not having enough time. You may also have an internal conflict because you don't feel you are doing a good enough job as a parent.

Choose one conflict to write about. Make notes on how this conflict makes you feel. If it is an external conflict, write down conversations you have had (or imagined having) with the other people involved.

Drafting

Turn your conflict into a story. You can solve the conflict any way you like. You can make the characters say and do whatever you want them to. Giving the main character a name other than your own may help remind you that this is fiction, not fact. Remember to describe the characters and the setting. Decide what the climax of your story will be.

Revising

Variety makes writing more interesting. Vary your sentence length, and use statements, questions, and exclamations.

Editing

Use commas between each item in a list. Example:

■   Brayton screamed, fell, and groaned.

Theme

Writers often use specific characters and events to make statements about life or about human nature. This message about life is called the **theme** of a story. Often a story's theme can be interpreted in more than one way.

We all tend to draw conclusions about life from our experiences. For example, if you often see newspaper articles about criminals getting caught, you may conclude that crime does not pay. If your coworker gets a raise and you do not, you may conclude that life is not fair. If you read about a movie star's painful divorce, you may conclude that money cannot buy love. All of these conclusions could be used as the themes of short stories.

For more examples, look at the stories you have read so far in this unit. The theme of "The Eyes of Mr. Lovides" is that our impressions about other people can be mistaken. Mr. Lovides is not the kind of person that Joey thought he was. The theme of "Tom Sawyer, the Pirate" is that everyone needs to feel loved. The theme of "An American Twenty" is that money has a powerful influence over people's lives. The theme of "The Man and the Snake" is that fear can be deadly.

Usually you have to infer, or figure out, the theme of a story. To do this, ask yourself, "What lesson about life did I learn from this story?"

◆ **As you read "Just Rewards," think about the theme.**

Just Rewards

George blew on his hands and pulled the cardboard up to his chin. He had been sleeping on the corner of Elm and Oak for a week now. He was getting used to never taking a shower and never getting enough to eat. Now that winter was here, how would he get used to always being cold? He'd just have to get up and move around.

George walked over to the appliance store on Fourth Street, where they left the TVs on all night. He watched in a daze of hunger and tiredness. Suddenly he recognized a face on the news. It was Martin Murk, his old boss.

Murk had owned the investment firm George used to work for. Murk cheated thousands of old people out of their life savings and was sentenced to five years in jail. The company folded, and George was out of a job. He had drifted for a while, finding work here and there. His last job had been washing dishes in a restaurant. They let him go because business was so bad, and that is when he wound up on the street.

Now George watched in disbelief as his thief of a boss was released from jail after only ten months. He heard the words "time off for good behavior . . . model prisoner . . . community service." Then the reporter said, "Murk says he will be moving ahead with a new business plan, though he is not ready to give details of that plan to the public." George shook his head and shuffled back to his spot on the pavement. The place was over a heating vent, so he did not want to lose it.

◆ **Answer this question about the story "Just Rewards."**

What are some of the truths about life that are shown in this story?

_____

_____

_____

The theme of the story can be expressed in a variety of ways. Here are some possibilities:

Homelessness often happens because of bad breaks.
Life is not fair.
Justice is only for the rich.

Strategy: Understanding the Theme

- Decide what lessons the characters learn about life.
- Ask yourself, "What did I learn from this story?"
- Put the writer's message in your own words.

Exercise

This mystery story is told by Dr. Watson, a good friend of Sherlock Holmes. It takes place in England in the early 1900s. Watch for the clues as you read!

Read the story and complete the exercise.

The Adventure of the Three Students

Adapted from the story by Sir Arthur Conan Doyle

Mr. Soames, a tutor at the College of St. Luke's, was upset. "Mr. Holmes," he began, "we have had a bad incident at St. Luke's. The scholarship examination begins tomorrow. The winner will receive a large sum of money. Today the Greek exam arrived from the printers. It was my job to read the exam carefully. I had to be sure it was correct. I left the exam on my desk when I went away for an hour to have tea with a friend.

"When I returned, I saw a key in my door. At once, I called my servant, Bannister. He had carelessly left it there. I immediately saw that someone had gone through my papers. One page was lying on the floor, one was near the window, and the third was where I had left it.

"Bannister denied looking at my papers. He was very upset, and he collapsed in a chair. I found several shreds from a pencil that had been sharpened. Evidently the rascal copied the paper, broke his pencil, and needed to put a fresh point on it. I also found a scratch on my writing table. And on the table was a small ball of black clay, with specks of sawdust in it. Please help me, Mr. Holmes! If I don't find the man, the examination must be postponed."

Holmes and I went with Mr. Soames to the college. He lived on the ground floor of an old college building. Three students lived on the upper floors. "Where is Bannister?"

Mr. Soames was upset. "He was ill, poor fellow. I left him in that chair," he said.

Holmes began looking at the papers. "He must have copied the first page, tossed it down, and then picked up the second page. When you returned, he left VERY quickly." Then Holmes opened the door to the bedroom. "What's this?" he asked, picking up some clay. "Your visitor must have been in your bedroom too."

"Do you mean he was there while I was talking to Bannister?"

Holmes nodded his head. "Do you suspect one of the students who live here?"

"I will tell you about the students. On the lower floor is Gilchrist, a fine scholar and a good athlete. He plays on the rugby and cricket teams, and he does hurdles and long jump. He is hardworking, and he will do well on the exam. On the second floor lives Daulat Ras, a quiet Indian fellow. He is a good student, though Greek is his weak subject. The top floor belongs to Miles McLaren. He is a brilliant fellow—when he chooses to work. But he has been wasting his time all term."

Holmes wanted to talk with each of the students. We went with Soames to visit Gilchrist and the Indian in their rooms. However, when we knocked at the door of the third student, an angry voice roared, "I don't care who you are! I don't have time for anyone."

"A rude fellow," said Mr. Soames.

Holmes's response was a curious one. "Can you tell me his height?" he asked.

"I cannot say. He is taller than the Indian, but not so tall as Gilchrist. I suppose about five feet six."

"That is important," said Holmes. "And now, Mr. Soames, good night."

Mr. Soames cried out in surprise. "Mr. Holmes, don't leave yet! Tomorrow is the examination."

"I shall drop round early tomorrow."

The next morning Holmes was out of bed at six. He put in two hours of work. At eight o'clock, Holmes came into my room. He held out his hand. There lay three pieces of black clay. "Come along, Watson. Let's go. We need to get Soames out of his pain."

The tutor was very upset when we found him. The examination would soon begin, and he didn't know what to do. "Thank Heaven you have come! I was afraid you had given up. What am I to do?"

"You must go on with the exam."

"Do you know who the rascal is?"

"I think so. But to keep this matter to ourselves," Holmes said, "we must set up our own small court. Call for Bannister!"

Bannister entered, obviously surprised and afraid. "Now, Bannister," said Holmes, "tell us the truth about yesterday's incident."

The man turned white. "I told you everything."

"I have a question for you. When you sat down on that chair yesterday, were you hiding something?"

"Certainly not."

"Mr. Soames, please ask Gilchrist to come here."

LANGUAGE Tip

Sherlock Holmes was not a real person. However, his name is known around the world. His statue stands outside an underground train station in London.

When Gilchrist arrived, his troubled eyes glanced at each of us. "Now, Mr. Gilchrist," said Holmes, "we are quite alone here. You can tell us the truth about what you did yesterday."

The young man looked with horror at Bannister. "No, no, Mr. Gilchrist, sir. I never said a word—never one word!" cried the servant.

"Gilchrist, you have given yourself away," said Holmes. The student began to sob. "Everyone makes mistakes," said Holmes kindly. "You are not a criminal. Shall I tell Mr. Soames what happened?

"Mr. Soames, you said no one knew the papers were here. I examined your window to see how tall a man needed to be to see the papers on the table. I am six feet tall. Anyone shorter could not have seen the papers.

"This is what happened. Glichrist spent his afternoon at the athletic grounds, practicing the long jump. He returned carrying his jumping shoes, which—as you are aware— have sharp spikes. As he passed your window, he saw the papers. Then he saw the key that had been left in the door. Suddenly he decided to enter and look at the papers.

"When he saw the exam papers, he put his shoes on the table. Gilchrist, what did you put on the chair?"

"Gloves," said the young man.

"Then," Holmes continued, "he took the pages and began to copy them. Suddenly he heard the door open. He picked up his shoes and darted into the bedroom, scratching the table with his spiked shoes. The clay came from the shoes. A second piece fell in the bedroom. This morning I walked to the athletic grounds. Here is some clay from the jumping-pit."

"Mr. Gilchrist, have you nothing to add?" cried Soames.

"Yes, sir, I have. I have a letter here, Mr. Soames, that I wrote to you early this morning when I could not sleep. I wrote it before I knew anyone had discovered what I had done. My letter says I will not sit for the examination. I am going to South Africa at once to accept a position with the **Rhodesian** police." Then he pointed to Bannister. "This man set me on the right path."

"Come on, Bannister," said Holmes, "can you tell us the reasons for your actions?"

"It was simple, sir. Long ago, I was the butler for this gentleman's father. I never forgot my old employer. I kept my eye on his son here at St. Luke's. Well, sir, when

---

Rhodesia: a country in southern African, known today as Zimbabwe

I came into this room yesterday, the first thing I saw was Mr. Gilchrist's gloves on that chair. I flopped down, staying there until Mr. Soames left to find you. Then out came my poor young master. He confessed all to me. Wasn't it natural that I should speak to him as his dead father would have done? I wanted to make him understand that what he had done was wrong. Could you blame me, sir?"

"No, indeed," said Holmes. "Well, Soames, I think we have cleared up the problem., and our breakfast is waiting for us. Come, Watson! As to you, Gilchrist, I trust that you will have a bright future in Rhodesia. You have fallen low. Let us see in the future how high you can rise."

PART A

Circle *T* if the statement is true or *F* if it is false.

T F **1.** Soames is upset because he thinks a student is cheating on the exam.

T F **2.** McLaren copies the exam because he has not studied during the term.

T F **3.** Holmes figures out that a short student would have had the easiest time hiding in the bedroom.

T F **4.** McLaren is angry when Holmes knocks on his door because he does not want to be disturbed.

T F **5.** The story's theme is that people sometimes do wrong but they can learn from their mistakes.

T F **6.** The story's theme is that solving a crime requires the best detective.

T F **7.** Bannister has known Gilchrist for a long time.

T F **8.** Bannister is trying to help Gilchrist win a scholarship.

T F **9.** Bannister helps Gilchrist because the student once helped him.

T F **10.** Sherlock Holmes wants to see the guilty student punished.

PART B

Answer the questions in the space provided.

1. What is the main coflict in this story? Is it internal or external?

   _____

   _____

2. How do you know that Gilchrist has an internal conflict?

   _____

3. Why does Holmes ask Gilchrist, "What did you put on the chair?"

   _____

   _____

4. Explain what Holmes means when he says, "You have fallen low. Let us see in the future how high you can rise."

   _____

   _____

5. What is the climax of this story?

   _____

   _____

6. State the theme of the story in your own words?

_____

Check your answers on pages 165–166.

Writing Workshop

Prewriting

The theme of "The Adventure of the Three Students" is that people can learn from their mistakes. Think of situations where you knew that what you had done was not right and you learned a lesson from the experience. Then choose one situation to write about. Make notes about the situation in which you had to make a choice. Who was the other person involved in the conflict?

Drafting

Write one or more paragraphs describing how you learned a lesson about right and wrong. You do not have to state the theme at the end of your story, but your readers should be able to understand the lesson about life that you are sharing.

Revising

Ask a partner to read your story. Have your partner look carefully to see that all events have been described in time order. Add time-order clues such as _first, later, then, afterwards,_ and _finally_ to help the reader follow the order of events.

Editing

Check that apostrophes used to show possession are in the correct place. For a singular noun, add an apostrophe and an _s_ (day's, Herbert's, house's). For plural nouns, add an apostrophe (robbers', companies', the Alaskans').

Review – Reading Short Fiction

O. Henry is a famous American short story writer. His stories often have a surprise ending. What happens to Soapy that you don't expect?

Read the story. Then circle the best answer for each question.

The Cop and the Anthem

Adapted from the story by O. Henry

On his bench in Madison Square, Soapy moved uneasily. Wild geese were honking high overhead, and a dead leaf fell on his lap. Winter is near at hand. Soapy realized the time had come for him to find a place for winter. His ambitions were not of the highest. There were no thoughts of Mediterranean cruises. Three months on the **Island**[1] was what his soul craved—three months of food and bed and good company.

For years, Blackwell's had been his winter quarters. Just as other New Yorkers bought their tickets to Palm Beach, Soapy made his arrangements for his annual trip to the Island. The time had come. Three Sunday newspapers no longer kept him warm. So the Island loomed big and timely in Soapy's mind.

Soapy set about accomplishing his desire. There were many ways of doing this. The most pleasant was to dine at some expensive restaurant. Then, after declaring that he had no money, he would be handed over to a policeman.

Soapy left his bench and strolled out of the square. He turned up Broadway and halted at a glittering café. He had confidence in himself. He was shaven, and his coat was decent. If he could reach a table in the restaurant, success would be his. A roasted duck would be great—with wine, coffee, and a cigar. The bill would not be so high, yet the meal would leave him filled and happy for the journey to his winter home.

But as Soapy set foot inside the restaurant door, the head waiter's eye fell upon his frayed trousers and worn-out shoes. Strong and ready hands sent him back to the sidewalk.

Soapy turned off Broadway. He needed to find another way to the Island. At the corner of Sixth Avenue, electric lights lit up a shop window. Soapy took a stone and

---

[1]**Island:** Blackwell Island was the site of a state prison in New York City from 1797 to 1934.

dashed it through the glass. People came running, with a policeman in the lead. Soapy stood still. He smiled at the sight of the policeman's brass buttons.

"Where's the man that done that?" asked the officer excitedly.

"Don't you think I might have had something to do with it?" said Soapy. He sounded friendly, as someone who has just met good fortune.

The policeman refused to accept Soapy's suggestion. Men who smash windows do not remain to talk with the law. They take to their heels. The policeman saw a man half way down the block running to catch a car. He ran after the man. Soapy moved along. Twice unsuccessful.

Nearby was a simple restaurant. People who went there had large appetites and small purses. Soapy went in. He sat down and ate beefsteak, pancakes, doughnuts, and pie. And then he told the waiter that he didn't have a coin. "Now, get busy and call a cop," said Soapy. "And don't keep a gentleman waiting."

"No cop for you," said the waiter. Then two waiters threw Soapy out on the pavement. Arrest seemed but a rosy dream. A policeman who stood two doors away laughed and walked down the street.

Five blocks Soapy traveled before his courage permitted him to try again. This time he seemed to have an easy opportunity. A young woman was gazing at a display window. Two yards away a large policeman with a stern face leaned against a fire hydrant.

Soapy planned to make a pass at the woman. He straightened his tie and moved toward the woman. He made eyes at her, smiled, and started talking to her. Soapy saw that the policeman was watching him. The young woman moved away a few steps. Soapy followed, boldly stepping to her side, raised his hat and said, "Ah, there, Bedelia! Don't you want to come and play in my yard?"

The policeman was still looking. If the woman raised a finger, Soapy would be en route to the Island. Already he imagined he could feel the cozy warmth of the station-house. But the woman stretched out her hand, catching Soapy's coat sleeve.

"Sure, Mike," she said joyfully. "I'd have spoke to you sooner, but the cop was watching."

With the young woman holding onto his arm, Soapy walked past the policeman. He seemed doomed to liberty.

At the next corner, he shook off his companion and ran. He halted in the district where women in furs and men in greatcoats moved gaily in the wintry air. A sudden fear seized Soapy. He worried that some dreadful magic was making it impossible for him to be arrested. When he saw another policeman, he decided to get himself arrested for "disorderly conduct." Soapy began to yell, dance, howl, rave, and otherwise disturb the peace.

The policeman turned his back to Soapy and remarked to a citizen, "It's one of them **Yale lads**[2] celebrating their win over the Hartford College. Noisy; but no harm."

Soapy stopped his racket. Would no policeman ever lay hands on him? The Island seemed impossible to reach. He buttoned his thin coat against the chilling wind.

In a cigar store he saw a well-dressed man lighting a cigar. The man had set his silk umbrella by the door. Soapy stepped inside, picked up the umbrella and walked off with it slowly. The man followed hastily.

"My umbrella," he said, sternly.

"Oh, is it?" entered Soapy. "Well, why don't you call a policeman? There stands one on the corner."

The umbrella owner slowed his steps. The policeman looked at the two curiously.

"Of course," said the umbrella man—"that is—well, you know how these mistakes occur—if it's your umbrella, I hope you'll excuse me—I picked it up this morning in a restaurant—I hope you'll—"

"Of course it's mine," said Soapy, viciously.

The ex-umbrella man walked away. The policeman hurried to assist a tall blonde across the street.

Soapy walked eastward. He tossed away the umbrella. He muttered against the men who wear helmets and carry clubs. Then, on an unusually quiet corner, Soapy came to a standstill. Here was an old church. Through one window, a soft light glowed. The organist loitered over the keys, making sure of his mastery of the Sunday **anthem**.[3]

The moon was above, bright and quiet. Sparrows twittered. Soapy knew the anthem that the organist was playing. He remembered it from the days when his life contained such things as mothers and roses and friends. The old church brought a sudden and wonderful change in Soapy's soul. He thought about the pit he had fallen into.

Soapy's heart responded to this new mood. Suddenly he had a strong desire to pull himself up. He would make a man of himself. He would conquer the evil that was in him. There was time; he was young. Those solemn but sweet organ notes had set up a revolution in him. Tomorrow he would go find work. He would be somebody in the world. He would—

Soapy felt a hand laid on his arm. He looked quickly around into the broad face of a policeman. "What are you doing here?" asked the officer.

"Nothing," said Soapy.

"Then come along," said the policeman.

"Three months on the Island," said the Judge in the Police Court the next morning.

---

[2]**Yale lads:** students from Yale University
[3]**anthem:** a hymn sung at church

1. What have you learned about the main character?
   (1) He's a successful business man.
   (2) He always lives in the park.
   (3) He just got fired from his job.
   (4) He wears worn-out clothes.

2. Why does Soapy break the store window?
   (1) He wants what is in the store.
   (2) He thinks this will get him arrested.
   (3) He wants to find a place to sleep inside the store.
   (4) He hopes to get the woman's attention.

3. What can you tell about the main character from the story?
   (1) He is clever.
   (2) He is violent.
   (3) He is very old.
   (4) He is lonely.

4. What is the setting of the story?
   (1) a prison
   (2) a large city
   (3) a small town
   (4) a church

5. What is the climax of the story?
   (1) Soapy makes a plan for getting arrested.
   (2) Soapy refuses to give back the umbrella.
   (3) Soapy hears church music.
   (4) Soapy gets arrested.

6. Who is Soapy's external conflict with?
   (1) the police officers
   (2) his mother
   (3) the Judge
   (4) the woman by the store window

7. What is Soapy's internal conflict just before he is arrested?
   (1) He wants to be more violent.
   (2) He fears another winter in prison.
   (3) He wants to change his life.
   (4) He worries about his mother.

8. What is the theme of the story?
   (1) Everyone deserves a warm bed.
   (2) Be careful what you wish for.
   (3) You can't control your future.
   (4) Going to jail is not always bad.

9. What does this sentence mean: "He muttered against the men who wear helmets and carry clubs."
   (1) Soapy does not think that police need helmets and clubs.
   (2) Soapy fears the police.
   (3) Soapy is mad at the police.
   (4) Soapy wants to be a policeman.

10. Soapy is like Tom in "Tom Sawyer, the Pirate" in that
    (1) they both live in big cities
    (2) they both wish their lives were different
    (3) they are both homesick
    (4) they are both young boys

Check your answers on page 165.

Posttest

The Posttest will help you check how well you have learned the reading skills in this book. You should take the Posttest after you have completed all the exercises in this book.

You can check your answers on page 156. Then fill out the Posttest Evaluation Chart on page 155. The chart will tell you which sections of the book you might want to review.

Do you sometimes have trouble sleeping? What can you do to help solve this problem?

Read the passage and answer the questions.

Desperately Seeking Sleep

You have had a rough day, the kind you see in headache commercials. You come home and eat a big dinner. Then you feel the need for a nap. To wake up, you drink a cup of coffee. At bedtime, you toss and turn for hours. Every time you doze off, a car alarm sounds, your spouse snores, or your neighbors crank up their stereo. Finally, you drift off, but minutes later your alarm clock rings.

Most people need to sleep about eight hours to feel their best, so it is worth breaking bad habits to improve your quality of sleep. What can you do? First, eat sensibly. A big meal keeps you up at night. An empty stomach does too. Second, instead of taking a nap, try to fight that tired feeling by exercising. You will get more done in the evening, and you will be ready to sleep when you get into bed. Third, avoid caffeine, especially in the evening.

Noise at night is a problem, especially if you live in a city. Try earplugs. Try to go to bed at the same time every night, even on weekends. Develop a routine. Do the same things in the same order each night before bed, until falling asleep becomes part of your nightly habit.

1. What is the main idea of the passage?

   (1) Life is exhausting.
   (2) There are things you can do to sleep better.
   (3) Caffeine will kill you.
   (4) You should go to bed at the same time every night.

2. Which would be the best title for this passage?

   (1) Wake Up and Smell the Coffee
   (2) Sleep Problems Are Leading Cause of Crime
   (3) Never Marry a Snorer
   (4) How to Get a Good Night's Sleep

3. What can you do to sleep better?

   (1) Eat a sensible dinner.
   (2) Get enough exercise.
   (3) Develop a routine.
   (4) all of the above

4. How many hours a night does the average person need to sleep?

   (1) six
   (2) seven
   (3) eight
   (4) nine

5. What should you do if you feel tired before bedtime?

   _____

   _____

6. What substance should you avoid before bedtime?

   _____

Do you think jobs that hurt the environment should be cut? Or is it more important that people keep their jobs regardless of how those jobs affect the environment?

Read the passage and answer the questions.

Jobs Versus the Environment

Many people speak out against laws passed to protect the environment. They believe protecting nature means losing jobs, and these jobs are needed so families can be fed. For example, these people oppose laws written to protect the spotted owls living in Oregon forests. They think protecting forests means loggers will be out of jobs. They also oppose laws that would prevent tuna fishers from using nets. They think fishers will not be able to catch enough tuna to make a living. They object to laws requiring businesses to clean the air coming from their factories. They think these businesses should be spending their money on paying better wages.

Is this true? The evidence shows that the choices are more complicated. For example, if Oregon forests continue to be cut down, loggers will be out of jobs because there will be no more trees. Trees that are hundreds of years old will be gone forever. Cutting down trees would not only destroy the spotted owls. It would also weaken the economy because fewer tourists would visit the state.

The fishers using nets are wiping out the tuna population. If they continue to catch large numbers of fish, soon they will not be able to support themselves. And I believe most businesses can afford to invest to clean the air they are using. They need to help save the environment. How can you put a price on giving children a healthy world?

—Maria Gómez

7. Why do some businesspeople say we cannot save the environment?

    (1) Saving the environment would mean losing many jobs.
    (2) A growing economy is more important than clean air.
    (3) Spotted owls do not contribute anything to the world.
    (4) Pollution is just an imaginary problem.

8. Why would cutting down the old Oregon forests be bad for everyone?

    (1) Old trees would be lost forever.
    (2) Loggers would soon be out of work.
    (3) The state would earn less money from tourists.
    (4) all of the above

9. Which of the following statements is a fact?

    (1) Protecting nature means losing jobs.
    (2) Most businesses can afford to clean the air they are using.
    (3) Spotted owls live in Oregon forests.
    (4) You cannot put a price on giving children a healthy world.

10. Which of the following statements is an opinion?

    (1) It costs money to fight pollution.
    (2) Protecting nature means losing jobs.
    (3) Many trees in Oregon forests are hundreds of years old.
    (4) all of the above

11. Which statement from the passage shows a bias in favor of protecting the environment?

    (1) The fishers using nets are wiping out the tuna population.
    (2) I believe most businesses can afford to invest to clean the air they are using.
    (3) How can you put a price on giving children a healthy world?
    (4) all of the above

12. What two points of view are described in this commentary? _____

    _____

    _____

Did you ever get a reaction from someone that was different from what you expected?

Study the cartoon and answer the questions.

13. What sport is the man watching on television? How do you know?

_____

_____

14. Why does "the born loser" rush to tell his wife about the game?

    (1) He wants her to calm him down.
    (2) He wants her to share his excitement.
    (3) He knows she will be fascinated.
    (4) He is too upset for words.

15. What can you infer, or figure out, about Gladys's attitude toward baseball?

    (1) She is a real fan.
    (2) She prefers basketball.
    (3) She supports her husband's interest in the game.
    (4) She finds baseball boring.

16. How does Gladys's reaction make her husband feel?

    (1) let down
    (2) relieved
    (3) excited
    (4) furious

What is being described? Which details help you understand what is happening?

Read the poem and answer the questions.

The Exchange

They handed her the folded flag to hold.
It lay against her breast and she was cold.
Her heart was bleak and **wrenched**[1] with unshed tears,
The **culmination**[2] of the weeks of fears.
5   A flag was used to lure away her son
To fight a war she heard would not be won.
He had come home in peace at last to stay
So now her fears could all be put away.

"He's the town hero," she heard someone brag
10 As they handed her the American flag.

—by Nola Plambeck

[1]**wrenched:** suffering
[2]**culmination:** end

17. How many verses does this poem have? _____ _____

18. Which pairs of words rhyme? _____ _____

19. What sense does line 2 of the poem appeal to? _____

20. Which line appeals to the sense of sound? _____

21. Is the speaker creating a sad tone or a mysterious tone? _____

22. What is the topic of this poem? _____

23. What does line 5 tell you about why the son went to war?

_____

24. What does line 8 tell you about the mother? _____

25. What was this flag used for before it was given to the mother? _____

Has your life turned out as you wished? Have you done the things you really wanted to do?

Read the passage and answer the questions.

A Man Told Me the Story of His Life

by Grace Paley

Vicente said: I wanted to be a doctor. I wanted to be a doctor with my whole heart.

I learned every bone, every organ in the body. What is it for? Why does it work?

The school said to me: Vicente, be an engineer. That would be good. You understand mathematics.

I said to the school: I want to be a doctor. I already know how the organs connect. When something goes wrong, I'll understand how to make repairs.

The school said: Vicente, you will really be an excellent engineer. You show on all the tests what a good engineer you will be. It doesn't show whether you'll be a good doctor.

I said: Oh, I long to be a doctor. I nearly cried. I was seventeen. I said: But perhaps you're right. You're the teacher. You're the principal. I know I'm young.

The school said: And besides, you're going into the army.

And then I was made a cook. I prepared food for two thousand men.

Now you see me. I have a good job. I have three children. This is my wife, Consuela. Did you know I saved her life?

Look, she suffered pain. The doctor said: What is this? Are you tired? Have you had too much company? How many children? Rest overnight, then tomorrow we'll make tests.

The next morning I called the doctor. I said: She must be operated immediately. I have looked in the book. I see where her pain is. I understand what the pressure is, where it comes from. I see clearly the organ that is making trouble.

The doctor made a test. He said: She must be operated at once. He said to me: Vicente, how did you know?

26. What do the tests *not* show about Vicente?

    (1) He is good at math.

    (2) He would be a good engineer.

    (3) He would be a good doctor.

    (4) all of the above

27. Why does Vicente agree to the job the teachers want him to have?

    (1) He thinks they are wiser than he is.

    (2) He wants to stay out of the army.

    (3) He faints at the sight of blood.

    (4) He has three children to support.

28. List at least three clues that tell you Vicente would be a good doctor.

_____

_____

29. Over what period of time does this story take place?

    (1) less than one day

    (2) one week

    (3) ten days

    (4) at least ten years

30. What is the setting at the end of the story?

    (1) the school

    (2) the army

    (3) the doctor's office

    (4) none of the above

31. How did Vicente know what was wrong with his wife?

    (1) He looked it up in medical books.

    (2) He remembered what he had studied about the human body as a teenager.

    (3) He knew where the pain came from.

    (4) all of the above

32. What is the climax of the story?

    (1) The tests say Vicente should be an engineer.

    (2) Consuela gets sick.

    (3) Vicente figures out what is wrong with Consuela.

    (4) Vicente learns every bone and organ in the body.

33. Do you think Vicente's ethnic background could have anything to do with the advice the school gives him? If so, how?

_____

_____

34. When the doctor first examines Consuela, what does he think is wrong with her? What clues tell you?

_____

_____

35. What is the conflict that Vicente has at the beginning of the story?

_____

_____

36. Which statement best states the theme of this story?
    (1) A good job is hard to find.
    (2) Decide for yourself what to do with your life.
    (3) It is wise to marry a man who has studied medicine.
    (4) Knowing how something works is not the same as being able to fix it.

Check your answers on page 156.

Posttest Evaluation Chart

Use the Posttest Answer Key on pages 156–157 to check your answers. Next, find the number of each question you missed. Circle that number in the Item Number column of this chart. Then write the number of correct answers you had for each skill. If you need more practice in any skill, refer to the chapter that covers that skill.

Chapter	Skill	Item Number	Number Correct
1	Main Idea	1, 2	
2	Details	3, 4	
3	Time Order	5, 6	
4	Main Idea and Reasons	7, 8	
5	Facts and Opinions	9, 10	
6	Detecting Bias	11, 12	
7	Making Inferences	13, 14, 15, 16, 24	
8	Form	17	
9	Rhythm and Rhyme	18	
10	Imagery	19, 20, 21, 22, 23	
11	Similes and Metaphors	25	
12	Characters	26, 27, 28	
13	Setting	29, 30	
14	Plot	31, 32, 33	
15	Conflict	34, 35	
16	Theme	36	

Posttest Answer Key

1. (2) The passage explains how a person can sleep better. Choices (1) and (3) exaggerate the facts. Choice (4) is a detail, not the main idea.

2. (4) Every paragraph is related to sleeping well. Choices (1) and (2) are not mentioned. Choice (3) relates to a detail, not the main idea.

3. (4) All three choices are mentioned in the passage.

4. (3) The average person needs to sleep about eight hours (paragraph 2).

5. Exercise instead of taking a nap (paragraph 2).

6. caffeine (paragraph 2), which is found in coffee, tea, colas, and chocolate

7. (1) Some people object to the cost of solving environmental problems. Choices (2) and (3) are not mentioned in the passage. Choice (4) is not true.

8. (4) All three effects are mentioned in the passage.

9. (3) This fact can be proved. Choices (1), (2) and (4) are opinions.

10. (2) This is an opinion. Not everyone agrees with it. Choices (1) and (3) are facts.

11. (4) All three statements use language that clearly shows the writer is in favor of protecting the environment.

12. The first point of view supports business. The second supports the environment.

13. Baseball; the man refers to pitching and to runs, hits, walks, and errors.

14. (2) The details of the cartoon show that the man is excited and wants his wife to share in the excitement.

15. (4) The wife's boredom is shown in frame 5 when she says, "So what?"

16. (1) He is not as excited as he was before. But frame 6 does not indicate he is relieved, excited, or furious.

17. two

18. hold/cold; tears/fears; son/won; stay/away; brag/flag

19. Touch; the reader can feel the folded flag and feel the cold.

20. In line 9, the reader can imagine hearing someone say those words.

21. Sad; words such as *cold, bleak,* and *tears* are all sad words.

22. the loss of young men in war OR a mother's sadness

23. The flag represents the country. The young man loved his country, so he went to war.

24. She would no longer worry about him. What she feared had already happened.

25. The flag was covering her son's coffin before it was given to her.

26. (3) The tests do not show whether he will be a good doctor. The tests do show that he is good at math (choice 1) and that he would be a good engineer (choice 2).

Posttest Answer Key

27. (1) In paragraph 6, Vicente says he thinks the teachers and the principal must be right.

28. The clues include the following: He knows every bone in the body. He knows how the organs connect. He wants to be a doctor with his whole heart.

29. (4) Vicente is in school at the beginning. Then he goes into the army, has a career, gets married, and has three children.

30. (3) The doctor is talking to Vicente, so the final paragraph takes place in the doctor's office.

31. (4) All three choices are mentioned.

32. (3) The most exciting point of the story is when Vicente, because of his knowledge about medicine, figures out what is wrong with Consuela.

33. It is possible the teachers think a Hispanic student will have difficulty getting into medical school.

34. The doctor thinks the illness may be caused by stress. He questions her about whether she has had too much company or has too many children. He does not take any tests the first day.

35. Vicente's conflict is with his teachers and the principal. He wants to be a doctor, but they insist he should be an engineer.

36. (2) The lesson about life that this story teaches is that you must make your own decisions in life.

Answer Key

Unit 1: Practical Reading

Chapter 1: Main Idea

Exercise 1, pages 6-7

1. Read all the instructions carefully before you use your new microwave oven.
2. how to cook broccoli for 2 minutes and 30 seconds at power level 5
3. Press 3, 2, and 0, then *Power*, then 7, and finally *Start*.
4. *Start*
5. It clears the display and allows you to start again.

Exercise 2, pages 8-9

1. c   4. f
2. e   5. d
3. a   6. b

Exercise 3, pages 10-11

Answers may vary. Use these answers as a guideline.

1. Juggling daycare and work schedules is hard to do.
2. Bob drops off their daughter at school, while Rosa takes their son to daycare before she goes to work.
3. Some employers offer job-sharing programs for working parents.
4. increased productivity, reduced absenteeism and tardiness, less staff turnover, greater job satisfaction

Chapter 2: Details

Exercise 1, pages 14-15

Answers may vary. Use these answers as a guideline.

1. When an emergency arrives, it may be too late to gather the supplies that you need.
2. juice boxes, peanut butter, granola bars, canned meat, canned fruit
3. radio and flashlight
4. in a covered plastic box or a large backpack
5. Make an emergency kit now.

6. You may never need this emergency kit, but it is wise to be prepared.

Exercise 2, pages 16-17

Answers to questions 2–4 may vary. Use these answers as a guideline.

1. I Scream for Ice Cream (108) and Pizzarific (109)
2. Walk forward, going to the right around the benches. At Chocolate Dreams, turn right. The toy store is on the right, just before Troutman's Department Store.
3. Walk toward the center of the mall. Go to the right, around the benches. The ATM area is at the beginning of the next group of shops.
4. Turn right at the bench area. Then turn right again. Pizzarific is the first shop on the right.

Exercise 3, pages 18-19

PART A

1. k   6. j   11. m
2. f   7. a   12. g
3. n   8. i   13. l
4. b   9. d   14. c
5. h   10. e

PART B

1. d
2. e
3. b
4. c
5. a

Chapter 3: Time Order

Exercise 1, pages 22-23

1. get paint samples
2. measure the room
3. buy materials
4. cover furniture
5. put tape where needed
6. fill holes
7. paint
8. look for missed spots
9. clean up

Exercise 2, pages 24-25

1. (2) This detail is found in paragraph 3.
2. (3) This detail is found in paragraph 4.
3. (1) This detail is found in paragraph 3.
4. (4) This detail is found in paragraph 3.
5. (2) This detail is found in paragraph 5.

Exercise 3, pages 26-27

1. 20 minutes
2. the cool-down period
3. 140 to 160 beats per minute
4. at least 5 minutes
5. 70 beats per minute

Unit 1 Review—Practical Reading, pages 28-29

1. (3) The passage focuses on this topic. Choices (1) and (4) are supporting details. Choice (2) is false.
2. (1) Choices (2), (3), and (4) are false.
3. (4) Choices (1), (2), and (3) are all true.
4. (2) Sentence 2 in paragraph 4 tells you this detail. Choices (1), (3), and (4) are false.
5. (2) Sentence 3 in paragraph 6 gives this detail. Choices (1), (3), and (4) are false.

Unit 2: Reading Nonfiction

Chapter 4: Main Idea and Reasons

Exercise 1, pages 34-35

1. (2) Choices (1) and (3) are given as reasons for the main idea. Paragraph 1 suggests that choice (4) is false.
2. (1) Paragraphs 2, 3, and 4 tell you why biking is booming. Choices (2) and (3) (discussed in paragraph 5) are not true.
3. (4) The shortage of bike paths is discussed in paragraph 5. Choice (1) is given as a reason for biking (in paragraph 4), choice (3) (in paragraph 3) is not true, and choice (2) is not discussed.
4. (3) The fact that more riders are using helmets is mentioned in paragraph 4.
5. (1) The drawback of cold and icy weather in the winter months is mentioned in paragraph 5.

Exercise 2, pages 36-37

Answers may vary. Use these answers as a guideline.

1. **Main idea:** Closed captioning is useful for a number of reasons.
   Reasons: It is helpful for deaf or hard-of-hearing viewers, for people learning English, in noisy places, and in quiet places.
2. **How:** Captioning used to be open (visible to all). Now it is closed (viewers see captions only when they choose that option).
   Why: Viewers who did not need the captions complained that captioning took up too much space on the screen.
3. The decoders were needed to enable TVs to show the captions.
4. A new law required that decoders be built into TVs manufactured after 1992. Now all viewers can decide whether they want to use closed captioning.

Exercise 3, pages 38-39

1. Americans do not get enough sleep.
2. People worry about personal or work problems; many watch TV; some surf the Internet; some have insomnia.
3. **Main idea:** Not getting enough sleep can have serious effects.
   Reasons: Sleepy people are grumpy and cranky; they have trouble concentrating; their actions do not make sense; they do poorly at work; they are bad drivers; they fall asleep driving; they may be responsible for road rage.
4. These changes can help people get the sleep they need.

Chapter 5: Facts and Opinions

Exercise 1, pages 42-43

1. O	6. F
2. F	7. O
3. O	8. F
4. O	9. O
5. F	10. O

Answer Key

1. 3   3. 3
2. 1   4. 2
5. Plates are great.
6. Answers will vary.

1. 1   3. 2
2. 3   4. 4

Chapter 6: Detecting Bias

PART A
1. a. look, feel, and play basketball like a pro
   b. extra jumping power for those slam-dunk shots
   c. for the good times in your life
2. a professional basketball player
PART B
1. a. I wouldn't be where I am today if I didn't wear Smooth Air shoes.
   b. I protect them with Smooth Airs.
   c. They feel comfortable.
2. (1), (5) The ad does not suggest the other choices.

Answers will vary. Use these answers as a guideline.
1. The park will be a great improvement to the city.
   The park will cost too much money.
2. This is an opinion. Predictions about the future are always opinions.
3. Descriptions: They must not be proud of the city. They are stick-in-the-muds who do not like change. They prefer ugly parking lots.
4. Phrases such as *stick-in-the-muds* and *ugly parking lots* use loaded words. They show that the writer is biased.

1. B   5. B
2. B   6. B
3. F   7. B
4. F   8. F

Chapter 7: Making Inferences

1. Statements (1), (3), and (4) are facts. Without understanding these ideas, the reader will not understand the cartoon.
2. (2) No serious dieter eats candy and diet pills at the same time. In addition, this woman seems to be a "couch potato" (someone who sits and watches TV instead of exercising).
3. (3) The sun is so hot that it can cook meat.
4. (3) This cartoon is about global warming. It warns people that Earth is gradually getting warmer.
5. (2) The year 2050 is in the future. The cartoonist believes that Earth will be much warmer in 40 years.

1. morning
2. in front of her house
3. getting the morning newspaper
4. the titles of important articles in the newspaper
5. Possible answer: The more important the news, the larger the headline. Bad news often has the biggest headline. When the headlines are not big, the news is not so bad.
6. the man's secretary
7. call a computer technician to fix his computer
8. smashed his computer to bits
9. Possible answer: The man was so frustrated that he couldn't wait for help.

Exercise 3, page 62

1. **S** Janis says, "That's a pretty salad."
2. **I** Janis's expression as she says "Yeah, yeah, I know" shows she doesn't really agree that all great chefs are men.
3. **S** When Janis tells Arlo how pretty his salad is, he replies, "But of course!"
4. **S** The child's question is shown in frame 3 of the cartoon.
5. **I** The writer is emphasizing that men and women are not paid equally for the same work. In fact, they are given different titles for the same work.
6. **S** Arlo states this in frame 2 of the cartoon.
7. **I** Arlo's self-confidence is suggested by his comment "But of course!"
8. **I** This can be inferred because the child is asking a question about Janis and Arlo's conversation.

Unit 2 Review—Reading Nonfiction, pages 64–65

1. (2) This is discussed in paragraph 1.
2. (4) This is discussed in paragraph 1. The other statements are all opinions.
3. (3) This statement may not be true for all administrative assistants. The other statements are all facts that can be proved.
4. (4) This bias is shown throughout the article.

Unit 3: Reading Poetry

Chapter 8: Form

Exercise 1, pages 70–71

1. (4) All three choices describe the arrangement of words in the poem. The poem's form looks like a candy bar.
2. (1) The poem appeals to the reader's senses of sight and taste. Nothing in the poem relates to the sense of smell, hearing, or touch.

3. (2) The speaker says he feels like he has already had too much candy but he will have more anyway.
4. (4) These four ingredients are named in the poem.
5. (3) Snickers bars contain chocolate, peanuts, and caramel.

Exercise 2, pages 72–73

Answers for questions 5–7 may vary. Use these answers as a guideline.

1. seven (line 2)
2. the Golden Shovel (line 2)
3. five stanzas
4. two lines
5. Placing "We" at the end of the line makes the word seem more important. The speaker of the poem wants readers to understand that he and his friends are important.
6. The speaker is a young man in his late teens or early twenties. He is not well educated ("We real cool" is not a complete sentence). He probably wears cool clothes (line 3). He is leading a tough life (lines 7 and 8) and will probably not live long (line 10).
7. *Funny* and *happy-go-lucky* do not fit the poem. All other choices are possible.

Exercise 3, pages 74–75

1. (4) The capital letters form the smooth shape of a light bulb.
2. (3) The poet is appealing most to the sense of sight.
3. (1) The poet is having fun. He wants to entertain his readers and surprise them with his message.

Answer Key

Chapter 9: Rhythm and Rhyme

Exercise 1, pages 78-79
1. F Line 7 says "he grew old."
2. T There are no lines that are very long or very short.
3. F Many lines do not end with punctuation. The reader would slow a bit and then read on.
4. F The first two lines in the last verse do not rhyme.
5. T This pattern appears in all the stanzas of the poem.
6. F These words do not rhyme.
7. T He says "Ride, boldly ride" (line 22).
8. T Repeating words helps give a beat to the poem.
9. gallant
10. song *or* search
11. found
12. like
13. (2) "Sunshine" means happy times, and "shadow" means sad times.
14. (3) This knight is like many people who are always looking for something better than they have.

Exercise 2, pages 80-81
1. T 4. T
2. F 5. T
3. T 6. 3
7. the scoop that is lifted up
8. The scoop is like a mouth filled with food.
9. Its boom moves up so the dirt can be moved away.

Exercise 3, pages 82-83
Answers may vary. Use these answers as a guideline.
1. Lines 1 (gray), 2 (say), and 3 (day) rhyme. Lines 4 (beyond) and 6 (pond) also rhyme.
2. It changes from sad to happy. Verse 1 describes a sad, gray day. The rest of the poem describes how everyone (including the ducks) laughed when they saw what happened to Daddy.
3. These words probably stand by themselves so the reader will pause before telling what happens.

4. The lines at the beginning of each verse rhyme, and the lines at the end of each verse rhyme. The extra lines "WHEN" and "THEN" rhyme.
5. When people laugh very hard, they often slap their knees.

Chapter 10: Imagery

Exercise 1, pages 86-87
1. sight
2. hearing
3. touch
4. a snake moving through the desert
5. wind and animals
6. four
7. This poem is not a rhyming poem. None of the words at the ends of the lines rhyme.
8. The poet names the senses that he speaks about in the three previous verses—seeing, feeling, and hearing.

Exercise 2, pages 88-89
1. the cool sea breeze; the warm sand under the towel; the salty breeze in the speaker's ears
2. the quietness of the beach; the sound of the waves; Mom humming
3. a lullaby that sends a baby to sleep
4. three
5. None of the words at the ends of lines rhyme.
6. Everything the speaker senses at the beach makes him feel relaxed and happy.
7. Answers will vary.

Exercise 3, pages 90-91
1. Love is something with wings that flies around in the sky. It is described like a bird that is hunting.
2. a child crying (line 4); the world talking about happy things (lines 17 and 18)
3. sky/dry; pain/name (almost rhyme); flight/night; land/man (almost rhyme); things/wings
4. There is no such thing as a love that can fly around, and there is no possibility that the whole world will be happy and live in peace.

Chapter 11: Similes and Metaphors

Exercise 1, pages 94-95

Answers for questions 4 and 5 may vary. Use these answers as a guideline.

1. (2) The mother's advice about not giving up is given in lines 14–17. She wants her son to keep climbing.

2. (3) The long lines take a lot of breath to read, just as climbing some steps takes a lot of breath. Other lines (and other steps) are quick and easy.

3. (3) Lines 3–7 and 12–13 describe an old, dark stairway.

4. Most of the poem is about the mother's hard life. She says, "It's had tacks on it" (line 3), it's been "bare" (line 7), and there's been "no light" (line 13).

5. The mother's advice is encouraging, especially "don't you turn back" (line 14).

Exercise 2, pages 96-97

1. 3
2. 2
3. 1
4. Possible answer: In a filing cabinet, each piece of paper has a place in a folder. In an apartment house, each person has a room.
5. Busy people move in and out of little "cells" all day long.
6. lives/hives; comb/home

Exercise 3, pages 98-99

1. F   His eyes are compared to pearls that are in water.

2. T   His eyes glow *like* pearls. The word *like* is used in a simile.

3. F   He is like an eagle because of the way he sits and stares.

4. F   The cars are *like* ants. When *like* is used, the comparison is a simile.

5. T   Grandpa stares into nothing (line 3); he listens to the children as though he is hearing a faraway storm (lines 13–15).

6. T   Grandpa doesn't change. He wears his old hat (lines 4–5), and he spends his time thinking about years gone by (line 16). But the village has a different look—the land around it is no longer flat (lines 7–8).

7. F   There are no rhymes in this poem.

8. F   The poem has long lines and short lines. There is no regular beat in the poem.

9. T   The reader can imagine cars zooming. This image also appeals to the sense of hearing.

10. T   These are "good" images. They show that Grandpa is admired.

Unit 3 Review—Reading Poetry, pages 100-101

1. (2) The squirrel's greed is discussed in lines 6–9. Choices (1), (3), and (4) are all true, but they are not the main idea of the poem.

2. (4) Line 5 says, "And one gray squirrel named Joe."

3. (1) The difference in line lengths adds interest to the poem.

4. (3) *Snow* and *Joe* (lines 2 and 5) rhyme, and *seeds* and *breeds* (lines 3 and 4) rhyme.

5. (3) *Late* and *wait* (lines 7 and 9) rhyme, and *go* and *snow* (lines 10 and 11) rhyme.

6. (4) Choices (1), (2), and (3) are all images described in the poem.

7. (1) The idea that the squirrel is a bully is hinted at in lines 6–9.

8. (3) Line 1 mentions winter; lines 2 and 11 mention snow.

Unit 4: Reading Short Fiction

Chapter 12: Characters

Exercise, pages 106-111

1. (3) The three characters named and well described are Joey, Frank, and Mr. Lovides. Frank's new wife, the white-haired man who conducts the wedding, and the new man working the second counter are unnamed characters. Ralph is named (paragraph 15), but he has no part in the story.

2. (1) Joey finds Mr. Lovides frightening until the end of the story.

3. (3) Joey realizes that Mr. Lovides is *not* cruel or prejudiced. He wonders why he ever feared his boss.

4. (4) Frank says in paragraph 3 that Mr. Lovides's eyes are gentle and compassionate (caring).

5. (1) Frank's behavior toward Joey shows that Frank is warm and friendly.

6. (4) Throughout the story, Joey is shown to be shy and insecure. He is identified as Puerto Rican in paragraphs 13 and 23.

7. (3) Paragraphs 8 and 13 state that Joey likes sharp, dressy clothes.

8. (2) Joey loses a friend, but he gains confidence and pride.

9. (1) Frank is described in paragraph 14.

Answers may vary. Use these answers as a guideline.

10. (a) hiring Joey as second counterman when Ralph quits, (b) allowing Joey to attend Frank's wedding, (c) not criticizing Joey for being rude to one customer, and (d) promoting Joey to first counterman.

11. The way Joey speaks suggests that he is new to the country and still learning English: "Frank said he speak to you, ask you to let me off for his marriage. To be witness."

Chapter 13: Setting

Exercise, pages 114-119

1. Paragraph 15 says that the story takes place in late summer.

2. The story takes place in the Dominican Republic. Clues are the Dominican peso (paragraph 15) and the ten-peso coin (paragraph 43).

3. Clues include (a) sweat-dampened hair (paragraph 1), (b) a palm tree (paragraph 6), (c) tourists swimming in the ocean, (d) mangoes and oranges (paragraph 15), and (e) "It was too hot for the lady . . ." (paragraph 23).

4. Clues include (a) They live in a bark-walled house with no running water. (b) The children sell fruit to support the family. (c) Miguel earns money by doing chores for tourists. (d) The family raises chickens and a goat for food. (e) The $20 bill is a lot of money for them. (f) Juana can't afford to send her children to school.

5. No. Paragraph 21 says the American woman could not understand him.

6. Clues that one child is sick include (a) The smallest child is listless (paragraph 6), and the child whimpers and coughs (paragraph 48).
(b) The $20 will be used to buy medicine (paragraph 47).

7. No. She waits until he is asleep to give the $20 to Miguel (paragraphs 39–42).

8. School costs too much money (paragraphs 46 and 52).

9.

	Carreras Family	American Tourists
beach	*rocky, dangerous*	*smooth, soft, sandy, safe*
housing	bark-walled house, leaky roof, smell of sewage, near a dump, foul stream	pink hotel
ways each spends time	working: hauling water, washing clothes, milking goat, taking care of tourists	playing: fishing, swimming, parasailing, sunbathing
food	rice, goat milk, eggs, chicken	pizza, Coke

Chapter 14: Plot

Exercise, pages 122–127

PART A

Order of events: 2, 1, 6, 3, 5, 4

PART B

1. (1) Tom is the main character. The title, the opening paragraph, and the closing paragraph tell the reader that Tom is the most important character in the story.

2. (3) The second sentence of the story states the problem: "Nobody loved him."

3. (3) Although the school bell is mentioned, no action takes place at the school.

4. (1) Aunt Polly and Mrs. Harper are weeping and telling each other that their boys were really good boys, just mischievous.

5. (2) Steamboats would have been common on the Mississippi River 150 years ago. This fact helps you understand when the story took place.

6. (3) The event that solves the problem is Tom's being hugged by Aunt Polly at the end of the funeral. This is the climax of the story.

7. (1) Knowing that the villagers think they drowned is not a clue that the boys will go home. All the other choices show that the boys are unlikely to live forever on the island.

8. (4) Near the end of the story, Aunt Polly hugs Huck and calls him a "poor motherless thing."

9. (2) Aunt Polly calls Tom "mischEEvous." Mrs. Harper says Joe was "kind." And at the church the people think about how the boys always seemed like rascals.

10. Answers will vary.

Chapter 15: Conflict

Exercise, pages 130–133

PART A

1. He reads that the eye of a serpent is like a magnet. People get pulled to the eye and then they die.

2. Dr. Druring loves reptiles (snakes) and keeps them in the house.

3. It is unlikely that someone will die from seeing a stuffed snake.

PART B

1. (3) Only choice (3) is a problem in the story.

2. (1) Brayton moves forward inch by inch. He is afraid, but he wants to act bravely.

3. (2) Dr. Druring knows that his snakes can be very dangerous. He fears the worst.

4. (3) Brayton was, literally, frightened to death.

Chapter 16: Theme

Exercise, pages 136–141

PART A

1. T Soames thinks a student copied the exam he left on his desk.

2. F McLaren is not the student who copied the exam.

3. F Holmes does not mention the shortest student. He is concerned about a student tall enough to see in the window.

4. T McLaren is trying to study for the exam and does not want to be disturbed.

5. T This is the lesson about life that Holmes refers to at the end of the story.

6. F This is not the lesson about life that the story teaches.

7. T Bannister worked for Gilchrist's father many years ago, so he has known the young man for a long time.

8. F Bannister is upset about what Gilchrist has done. He is not trying to help him win a scholarship by cheating.

9. F Gilchrist's father was a good employer. Bannister wants to help young Gilchrist in the way a father would help a son do what is right.

10. F Holmes does not mention punishment. He thinks the student has learned a lesson.

PART B

Answers may vary. Use these answers as a guideline.

1. The main conflict in the story is external. Soames wants to find out which student is trying to cheat on the exam.

2. Gilchrist realizes that it is not right to cheat, so he decides not to take the exam.

3. Holmes thinks Bannister sat in the chair to cover something up, but he does not know what.

4. Cheating on an exam is a bad (low) thing to do. But in the future, Gilchrist can choose to do great things.

5. The climax of this story is when Gilchris is identified as the student who cheated and he says that he has decided he will not take the test.

6. People can learn from their mistakes.

Unit 4 Review—Reading Short Fiction, pages 142–145

1. (4) Soapy is described when he goes to the fancy restaurant.

2. (2) Soapy makes it clear that he is breaking the window only to get arrested. He does not want what is in the store.

3. (1) Soapy is full of ideas. He is a clever man.

4. (2) The story takes place in New York City. The prison Soapy wants to go to is in New York City.

5. (4) Soapy's problem is solved when he is arrested.

6. (1) The police are a problem for Soapy because they will not arrest him.

7. (3) The music from the church makes Soapy think about the life that he used to have. He decides he will change his life.

8. (2) Soapy has spent a long day wishing to get arrested. By the time he gets his wish, he has changed his mind.

9. (3) Soapy refers to the police as "men who wear helmets and carry clubs." He mutters against them because they are not doing what he wants them to do.

10. (2) Soapy wishes he had a warm place to spend the winter. Tom Sawyer wishes someone would love him.